THE
MAKING OF AMERICA
SERIES

LINDEN
NEW JERSEY

SOAPBOX DERBY, 1958. And they're off! This derby was sponsored by the Police Athletic League for the boys in Linden. (Courtesy Maureen Edwards.)

IN MEMORY OF
George Dorin, Wanda Green, Perry Leib, Rae Silverman, Sarah Lehmann, John Dobosiewicz, Raymond Wade, George Pencer, Robert Baldwin, Joseph, Emil, and Michael Pancurak.

HONORING
John T. Gregorio, Bernice Bedrick, Reed Fullerton, John Chabak, Paul Werkmeister, and Irene Pancurak.

FOR
Darren, Stephen, Kevin, and Chelsea Yeats.

THE
MAKING OF AMERICA
SERIES

LINDEN
NEW JERSEY

LAUREN PANCURAK YEATS

Best Wishes,
Lauren Pancurak Yeats
11/27/02

ARCADIA

Published by Arcadia Publishing,
an imprint of Tempus Publishing, Inc.
2 Cumberland Street
Charleston, SC 29401

Printed in Great Britain.

Library of Congress Catalog Card Number: 2001092149

For all general information contact Arcadia Publishing at:
Telephone 843-853-2070
Fax 843-853-0044
E-Mail sales@arcadiapublishing.com

For customer service and orders:
Toll-Free 1-888-313-2665

Visit us on the Internet at http://www.arcadiapublishing.com

LINDEN VOLUNTEER AMBULANCE COMPANY. *The squad proudly posed with its 1952 Cadillac ambulance. (Courtesy LVAC.)*

CONTENTS

ACKNOWLEDGMENTS

Every effort was made to provide interesting images as well as informative text for this book. This project was like a big jigsaw puzzle and many sources were sought to locate missing pieces. I enjoyed meeting so many people and wish to thank them for sharing memories of Linden. My deepest gratitude goes to the following for their help with information: Mayor John T. Gregorio, Carolyn Frees, Joseph Martino, Louis Di Leo, Esquire, Gary Maher, Linda Villani, Didon Villani, Richard and Kelly Koziol, John Koziol, Herb Worthington, Joseph W. Beviano II, Paul Mitro, Helen Pancurak, William Niemek, Bernice Bedrick, Harvey Thorn, Susan Shubeck, Roberta Specht, Reed Fullerton, Vivian Erickson, Reverend Dr. William Weaver, Samuel Friedman, Howard Silverman, Morton Weitzman, Walter and Stella Tylicki, Robert Croucher, Reverend Hobart C. Utter, Pastor Rob Taylor, Ted Rosenberg, Reverend Ronald A. Green, Andrea Amabile, Ceil Baldwin, Cindy Apalinski, Kenneth Krudys, John Kolibas, Stephen Hoptay, Cynthia Hoffman and Morris Leone, Alfred A. Volpe, Mimi Derrig, Bernard Plungis, Larry and Karen Lukenda, Ed and Jane Kushner, Ray Worrall, Barbara Chambliss, Colleen Nauta, Pat Malicher, Maurice Rakin, Vi DeGregorio, Bessie Smith, Gregory Martucci, Tyrone Givens, Bernice Flemmings, Donald Givens, Armando Canda, Arthur Boyd, Mattie Mathis, and the staff at the Linden, Elizabeth, and Newark Libraries for all of their help.

And for lending images for this work: Esther Leib, Ruth Rosenberg, Philip Okun, Shirley Stuewe, Peter Mazonas, Craig Wozniak, Bernie Wosniak, Alex Dimitrovski, Susan Hudak, James Iozzi, Blanche M. Brooks Hardy, Ruth Etta Apalinski, Frank Deubel, Mary Ann Dorin, Al Palermo, William Palermo, Robert Bersey, Paul Werkmeister, Charlotte Borst, Joan Drake, Patricia Sep, Steven Yesinko, Frank Taranto, Cindy Dudek, Doris Henel, Betty Lamont, Joseph Owens, Maureen Edwards, Mrs. Edward Flanagan, Richard Koziol, Allen Bedrick, Betty and Pat Banasiak, Edward Hering, the Linden Fire Department, The Linden VFW Post #1397, Robert Kastner, Georgette Dambrauskas LeNort, William Dougherty, and Robert Frazier. Special Thanks to: Charles Shallcross Jr., William and Ruth Frolich, Robert Fridlington, Charles Aqualina, Lester Sargent, Jean-Rae Turner, Richard T. Koles, Michael Yesenko, and Stephanie Laucius of the Union County Historical Society.

My thanks and personal admiration go to Mrs. Audrey Yeats and Mrs. Diana Kosiba for their help in retyping pages from microfilm research early in this project. I will always remember Secretary's Day 2001!

A big thank you to my mom Irene Pancurak and in-laws Richard and Audrey Yeats for their support and use of the facilities at Quality Graphics Center, Inc.; as well as to my children Stephen, Kevin, and Chelsea and my husband Darren for their constant love, patience, and support.

There were over 130,000 words originally in the manuscript. By the time it has reached you, it has been edited for space constraints by Arcadia Editor Christine Riley. My genuine thanks to her careful eyes.

LAUREN PANCURAK YEATS. Yeats spoke on behalf of the Union County Historical Society at the unveiling of the 1736 survey book at a special press conference presided by Mayor Chris Bolwage in the Elizabeth City Hall. Joseph Morss, whose tombstone can be seen on Stiles Street near Lower Road, authored the survey book. (Courtesy William Frolich.)

CAPTION ABBREVIATIONS

LBOE: Linden Board of Education
LFD: Linden Fire Department
LVAC: Linden Volunteer Ambulance Company
UCHS: Union County Historical Society
LY: Lauren Yeats

INTRODUCTION

We are caught in an inescapable network of mutuality, tied in a single garment of destiny. Whatever affects one directly, affects all indirectly.

~Dr. Martin Luther King, Jr.

"Home is where the heart is." Then to most of us, Linden is indeed home, for here are many hearts and here they choose always to remain, recalling their owners who stray to different ports from time to time.

This volume is intended as a tribute to Linden's rich heritage. It is my hope that it leaves you with an appreciation of the same. It was not to be one totally of facts and dates, but one of acts and people. I have tried to chronicle Linden's past for the future. May future generations find profit in what we have discovered and passed along as part of their heritage. The past may be writing the future, but you are in control of where it goes. Create a chapter that can fulfill your dreams and get to working on bringing it to life. Remember we are making history every day as we go about our way here. We should all make today count for the future generations! So here's to you, Linden.

1. The Early Days

The earliest inhabitants of this area were the Lenni Lenape, the "original people" of the Algonquin Indians. In 1524, Giovanni da Verrazano, an Italian navigator in the service of France, entered New York harbor through the strait that bears his name. Anchoring off Staten Island, he met native peoples who were most likely Lenape. In 1610, Captain Samuel Argall sailed up the Lenape River and named both the river and the people living on its banks "Delaware" in honor of his patron, Lord De la Warr. Europeans, therefore, referred to these people as the Delaware or Raritans. There were three tribes of the Lenape Indians, Munsee (Muncy), Unimi, and Unalachigo, and each spoke a different language.

The Lenape Indians had a government, customs, and their own religion. In 1836, Constantine Rafinesque published a book in which he described the Walam Olum, a series of pictograph-etched wooden sticks that were used by the Lenape to record their history. It begins with their departure from Siberia and follows their movement across North America until they reached the Atlantic Ocean. They were a tall people and lived in tents and long houses. Unfortunately, they did not survive long after the arrival of the Europeans, and conflict between the two cultures led to hostile wars. The Europeans' need to own the land, along with the diseases, guns, and alcohol they brought with them, created an impossible situation for the survival of the Lenape in their homeland. The federal census of 1890 was able to identify only 84 Indians in all of New Jersey. Today, the descendants of the Delaware Valley's Lenape tribes can be found scattered across reservations in Texas, Oklahoma, Wisconsin, and Ontario.

There was an extensive network of Native American paths over the land. The most notable locally was the Minisink Trail that led to the Native American village of Minisink. The trail in the Linden area encompassed Tremley Point Road, the Lower Road to Rahway, and an area of St. Georges Avenue to the west of the Rahway River. The path then crossed the Nomehagen at Branch Mills, touched Westfield east of Fairview Cemetery, and kept to the east of Ash Swamp (Tamaques). It also passed through Metuchen to the Raritan at Kents Neck opposite Sayreville.

After Verrazano, the next "official" contact for the Lenape was in 1609 when Henrik Hudson, employed by the Dutch East India Company to search for the

9

HENRY HUDSON
He landed on the shores of what would become Linden on September 6, 1609 and claimed the lands of the area for the Dutch. (Courtesy UCHS.)

Northwest Passage, arrived. The *Half Moon* explored the northeastern coast, eventually sailing into the mouth of a wide river near today's New York City. Hudson hoped the river (now known as the Hudson River) would provide a passage west to the Pacific Ocean. However, after traveling some 150 miles to the area now occupied by Albany, he found the river too shallow to continue. The records of the voyage relate numerous fights with the Indians and even the kidnapping of some for slaves, which may have influenced later relations between the natives and European settlers. After a short journey north, Hudson faced a possible mutiny of his crew. He turned his ship around and headed for a warmer climate.

The late Callahan J. McCarthy, a member of the Union County Historical Society and considered an expert on county history, once wrote, "It is fair to assume that it was on Sunday, September 6, 1609, that the eye of the white man first rested upon Linden and its vicinity." Hudson and a crew of 20 were exploring the waters around Staten Island when, on this date, five seamen came ashore to investigate the area now known as Linden. The following is an excerpt from Robert Juet's journal, held in the collections of the New York Historical Society, published in 1841:

Sunday, September 6, 1609
In the morning was fair weather, and our master sent John Colman, with four other men in our boat over to the north side to sound the other river, being four leagues from us. They found by the way shoal water two fathoms; but at the north of the river eighteen, and twenty fathoms, and very good riding for ships; and a narrow river to the westward between two islands. The land they told us were as pleasant with grass and flowers, and goodly trees, as ever they had seen, and very sweet smells came from them. So they went in two leagues and saw an open sea, and returned; and as they came back, they were set upon by two canoes, the one have twelve, the other fourteen men. The night came on and it began to rain so that their match went out; and they had one man slain in the fight which was an Englishman, named John Colman, with an arrow shot into his throat, and two more hurt. It grew so dark that they could not find the ship that night, but laboured to and fro on their oars. They had so great a stream that their grapnel would not hold them.

Monday, September 7, 1609
Was fair, and by ten o'clock they returned aboard the ship, and brought our dead man with them, whom we carried on land and buried, and named the point after his name. Colman's Point. Then we hoisted in our boat and raised her side with waste boards for defence of our men. So we rode still all night, having good regard to our watch.

After Hudson's return to Holland, the Dutch organized the United New Netherlands Company to manage this territory, which they named New Netherlands. By 1624, many Dutch settlers had arrived and claimed the land of "New Amsterdam" between the Connecticut and Delaware Rivers that Hudson had "discovered." These newcomers also tried to communicate with the Algonquins by teaching them Dutch.

The English Crown was quite unhappy with the Dutch acquisition of land in the New World, and so King Charles II of England presented the lands of New Amsterdam to his brother James, the Duke of York and Albany, to conquer for his own from the Dutch. The duke sent an expedition of Colonel Richard Nicholls and an army of 450 men on May 25, 1664 from England to seize New Netherlands, and they secured the surrender of Petrus Stuyvesant, the Dutch colonial governor, on September 8, 1664.

The area was renamed New Caeserea (New Jersey) and New York, in honor of George Carteret's defense of the Isle of Jersey in England, and James's title as Duke of York. The duke then appointed Nicolls governor of all the territories in North America. As governor, Nicholls advertised for settlers to improve the area, and soon, six Long Island men petitioned him to settle in Achter Kol (beyond the river). They were John Bayley, Luke Watson, Thomas Benydick, John Forster, and

Daniel and Nathaniel Denton. On September 30, 1664, Nicholls granted them permission to deal with the Native Americans for land from the Raritan River to Bound Brook, which encompassed the area today known as Union County. The men hired Captain John Baker, who spoke Dutch, as an interpreter, and the facts of the transfer are recorded in The Calendar of New Jersey's Records.

On October 28, 1664, the deed was signed by John Bayly, Daniel Denton, and Luke Watson; it also bore the marks of Mattano, Sewak Herons, and Warinanco. The sum, paid in goods, was estimated at £154. Nicholls confirmed the purchase on December 2, 1664, and on December 11, he made a deed granting the land to these settlers. The description included all the land between the Raritan and Passaic Rivers, and one provision stated that the grantees should "pay yearly to his Royal Highness, the Duke of York, or his assigns, a certain rent according to the customary rate of the country for new plantations." A copy of this indenture can be seen at the Union County Courthouse.

The settlers grew from 6 to 80 men who were known as the "Associates." They formed their community lines in accordance with the plan adopted in New England for mutual defense against the Lenape, which assured a compact settlement. Every settler was put on the same footing in regard to his homestead, and the plots of land were laid out on both sides of the "creek" (Elizabeth River), beginning with the first upland above the salt meadows and extending up the creek about 2 miles.

However, unknown to Nicholls and the Associates, James, the Duke of York and Albany, had granted Lord Berkley and Sir George Carteret the land from the Hudson to the Delaware Rivers and south to Cape May on June 23, 1664. According to the terms in their charter, Berkley and Carteret were the "Proprietors of the colony." Berkley and George Carteret appointed Philip Carteret as their governor, and he named the tract of land "Elizabeth towne," after the wife of Sir George. The Elizabeth Town tract contained a large area of land, and the Union County of today was part of that tract. The proprietors directed Philip Carteret to make conveyances for lands.

Governor Philip Carteret arrived in July 1665 at New York and came to Elizabeth Town with his servants and the first group of new settlers. For the first time, the Associates learned of the sale of the territory by the Duke of York to Berkeley and Carteret. Prior to their arrival, the duke had sold much of the land that the Associates had already settled. This created a conflict of land titles for years to come, and new titles were required to prove prior ownership by the Associates.

It seems that Philip Carteret paid little attention to the instructions he received from the proprietors and purchased an allotment from one of the Associates. He thereby became an Associate himself, but those who came with him did not meet with a cordial reception.

The question of quit rents (the payment of a half-penny per acre) did not assume importance until the time when payment was to be made. On March 25, 1670, many of the Elizabeth Town associates refused to pay, claiming that their

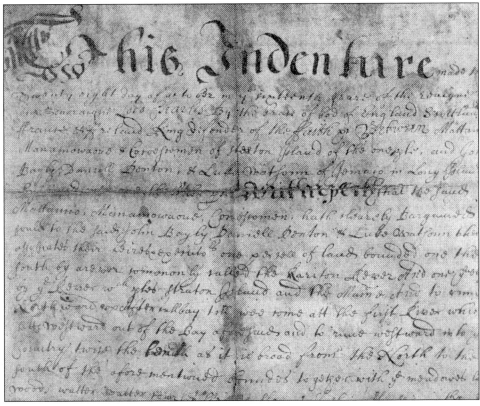

ELIZABETHTOWN DEED. The deed was photographed in 1964 when the state of New Jersey celebrated its 300th anniversary. (Courtesy UCHS.)

title antedated that of the proprietors. The Associates believed they had purchased the land in good faith, and Governor Nicholls confirmed their purchases.

In 1672, a war broke out between England and Holland, and the following year the Dutch recaptured their lost territory. Peace was established on February 9, 1674, and under the terms of the Treaty of Westminster, New Jersey was restored to England. Philip Carteret resumed the governorship. In 1674, Sir George Carteret gave instructions to Governor Philip Carteret to "collect rents or dispose of such lands and tenements for our best advantage."

When Sir George Carteret (fourth cousin to Philip Carteret) died in 1680, the property of East Jersey (which included Elizabeth Town) was sold to William Penn and 11 Associates for £3,400, and it was conveyed to them in 1682. Each of these 12 proprietors subsequently sold half of his prospective rights to a new proprietor, making 24 in all. In addition, Charles II granted these new proprietors the right of government.

To secure their rights, the people in Elizabeth Town applied for surveys and warrants from the royal governor. These surveys, however, did not end the matter. The associates were reluctant to give up their claims to large tracts of land. The attitude of the people finally drove the proprietors to take legal action. This dispute raged through the courts for nearly 100 years and seriously affected the Elizabeth Town families. The Revolution finally settled the matter.

The men in the area were predominantly farmers, but many other professions were also represented, including blacksmiths, carpenters, weavers, merchants, tailors, shoemakers, coopers, tanners, and brewers. There were also a few doctors, lawyers, goldsmiths, surveyors, and peddlers. But even the town merchants and peddlers were directly interested in the success of local crops.

Many of the colonial settlers in Elizabeth Town were Puritans and Presbyterians, who settled as far south as the Raritan. Many of them had come from Massachusetts but settled for a while in Long Island before coming to New Jersey. Others came directly from Massachusetts Bay and others from the British Isles. All were attracted by the liberal land policy of New Jersey's "Concessions and Agreement." According to this document, a man was given free land in proportion to the number of people he brought with him, including his family, servants, and slaves. The land policy also attracted many indentured servants. Slaves were numerous in the area well into the nineteenth century.

Slaves (both African American and Native American), redemptioners, and apprentices provided much of the labor supply for the colonies in their early history. Slaves were the most numerous in Bergen, Essex, Middlesex, and Monmouth Counties in East Jersey. The Rahway area was mostly under Quaker influence, so slavery there was sparse. During the Revolution, a great deal of agitation arose among New Jersey residents calling for the freeing of slaves.

Some families living in Elizabeth Town owned slaves, and newspapers of the day often contained items concerning the sale of slaves. The sale of a slave and other property belonging to the Winans family appeared in the July 5, 1780 edition of the *New Jersey Journal*.

> To be Sold, On Tuesday the 11th July, at 10 o'clock in the farm at the late dwelling-house of Isaac Winans, deceased, in Elizabeth Town, Rahway: one horse, cows, young cattle, sheep, hogs, wool, beds and bedding, Indian corn, many articles of house furniture, farming utensils, etc. etc. A stout negro at private sale. Articles will be made known at time of sale.

By 1798, slave traffic between New Jersey and other states was prohibited by the legislature. In 1804, the Act for the Gradual Abolition of Slavery was passed and resulted in the rapid decrease of the slave population. The act was enlarged in 1820 to provide for the faster abolition of slavery. After 1820, severe penalties were imposed on those involved in such trade. By 1840, there was but one slave in the borough of Elizabeth Town, which then included Linden.

2. Settlers of Linden

The most reliable statement of the names of the original Associates is found in *The Elizabeth Town Book (B)*, which was written some 50 years after the settlement of the town. Of the Associates listed, the following have been determined to have lived in what is now Linden: Nicholas Carter, William Johnson, Samuel Marsh, Robert Morse, Peter Morse (Morss), William Oliver, Humphrey Spinage, Thomas Thompson, Charles Tucker, Luke Watson, John Winans, Barnabas Wines, and Jonas Wood. Other Associates who owned land in Linden and probably lived here included Captain John Baker (Backer), Caleb Carwithy, William Cramer, Stephen Crane, Joseph Frazey, John Hinds, James Hinds, Abraham Shotwell, Michael Simpkin, and Nathaniel Tuttle. Records also indicate other settlers who were living in Linden during the seventeenth and early eighteenth centuries but were not members of the original Associates of Elizabeth Town. These settlers include William Broadwell, William Garthwaite, Joseph Halsey, Peter Noe, Abraham Roll, John Styles, Ephraim Terrill, and John Trembley. A brief biography of some of these men will provide a glimpse into life in their community during its early history.

William Broadwell, a cordwainer (shoemaker) by trade, is first mentioned living in the area of Wheatsheaf. Married to Mary Morse, Broadwell died on March 11, 1746, and his family later settled in New Providence.

William Garthewaite owned land in what are now Union, Cranford, and Linden. Born in England in 1677, he married Ann, the daughter of Maximilian Lawlon of France, in 1702 and may have come to New Jersey as early as 1703. He died on December 11, 1738, leaving at least two sons, Henry and James.

Joseph Halsey was born *c.* 1668. He came to the region at an early date from Southampton, Long Island and was living here by 1694. He bought from Derick Baker, the son of Captain John Baker, all the divisions accruing to a second lot right in Elizabeth Town. Halsey became one of the Associates in 1700, and lived near the Wheatsheaf Tavern. He married Elizabeth Haines, the sister-in-law of Richard Valentine, and the couple had 11 children: Sarah, Abigail, Rebecca, Joseph, Hannah, Phebe, Daniel, Isaac, Rachel, Deborah, and Nancy. Joseph Halsey died in April 1725.

Peter Noe, a grandson of immigrant Pierre Noue (who came to New York in 1663), owned large estates between Elizabeth Town and Woodbridge. Born in

1725, Noe had his homestead in the southwesterly section of Linden. It is also recorded that his son John married Catherine Trembley of Linden, a fact that tends to place this particular branch of Noes in Linden. The family name disappeared from Linden records *c.* 1890.

Jean Traubles (or John Trembly, or Trembley, or Tremley), a Huguenot, came to Elizabeth Town from Staten Island. He obtained about 200 acres by "land-pattent" from Governor Carteret but went on to purchase even more land. Traubles lived in the area that juts out into the Arthur Kill, and it became known as Trembly's Point, or Tremley Point as it is spelled today. In 1689, he married Marie (Mary), the daughter of Peter Nue (Noe), a French Huguenot refugee. Their son Peter operated a ferry from the "point" for many years. In a 1959 *Elizabeth Daily Journal* article, Mrs. Florence (Trembley) Crane, remembered putting on plays of the family's history at family reunions through the years. Her father David H. Trembley served as mayor of Rahway from 1918 to 1923, as did

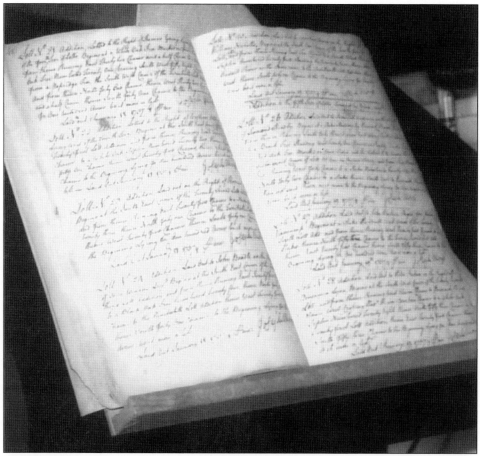

MORSS SURVEY MANUSCRIPT. Joseph Morss's manuscript was unveiled in February 2001. (Courtesy Frolich.)

Robert E. Henderson (the incumbent in 1959), who was also a Trembley. His grandmother was Elizabeth Trembley, an aunt of Florence Crane. The article continued, "Most of the former Trembly property was then occupied by Esso Standard Oil under a 99 year lease."

John Stiles (Styles) owned nearly 2 acres on the west branch of the Rahway River, according to the survey of December 20, 1739. In all probability, Stiles actually owned a great deal more acreage than listed. This family was quite extensive in Linden and had considerable land holdings in the vicinity of Stiles and Blancke Streets.

The Associates believed that they should strengthen their claim to the lands beyond the town of Elizabeth, and they appointed a group of men to survey the land west of Elizabeth Town to the foot of the Watchung Mountains. This naturally disturbed the proprietors, but they did little to enforce their claims. The Associates appointed Joseph Morss to make the surveys, which were compiled, upon completion, into *The Elizabeth Town Book (C)*. The manuscript contains the lot surveys for Elizabeth Town, New Jersey with the first entry made on November 8, 1736, when the Associates and "First Purchasers" of Elizabeth Town held a meeting and appointed Joseph Morss and his assistants to begin the surveying. The first lot was surveyed on December 27, 1736, and there are three later entries, indicating monies paid out, that were signed by important early members of the community, including Robert Ogden, who in 1763 was the Speaker of the New Jersey House, and in 1765 was a delegate to the Continental Congress. The survey covers a large area, including the "South Mountain" and land bordering the "Raway" and "Passaick" Rivers. Each entry describes the lot and boundaries and is signed by the surveyor, Joseph Morss. The Reverend Edwin F. Hatfield discusses *The Elizabeth Town Book (C)* in great detail in his *History of Elizabeth, New Jersey, Including the Early History of Union County*.

The Elizabeth Town Book (C) was returned to New Jersey in February 2001, after having been discovered in Pennsylvania and placed on an internet auction site. Rare books dealer Robert Grabowski of Lancaster, Pennsylvania had purchased the book some time prior, assuming it dealt with Elizabethtown, Pennsylvania. When he realized it was not the document he thought, he put it up for auction. The opening bid was $750. After being alerted to the auction, attorneys for the city and state went to Superior Court in Elizabeth and gained an order to stop the auction. After that, Grabowski donated the manuscript to the city. According to City Attorney William Holzapfel, First Assistant City Attorney Raymond Bolanowski and law clerk Donald Travisano went to Pennsylvania on February 14 to retrieve the book. "The book was determined to be a public historical document and property of the city of Elizabeth of important real-estate transactions between 1736 and 1757," said Karl Niederer, director of the New Jersey Division of Archives and Records Management. On Monday, February 26, 2001, the book was put on display at Elizabeth City Hall by Mayor J. Christian Bollwage, and the press conference drew an audience of eager city officials and history buffs.

"We are descended from a sister of the surveyor, Joseph Morss, so I feel a real affinity for the book," said Gary Maher, a trustee of the Genealogical Society of New Jersey, who said the manuscript can help with genealogical research.

William Frolich, a resident of Roselle and a member of the Union County Historical Society, described the book as follows:

> It is written in a very legible script, if you make allowances for the style of writing in 1700's. Words containing double "s" letters usually have the first "s" written as though it were an "f" The spelling of proper names is sometimes difficult to determine. Owners' names also have different spellings which are different from modern spellings. Elizabethtown was also written as Elizabeth Town or Elizabeth Towne. A prominent name in early Elizabeth Town varied even then. "Hatfield" was frequently spelled as "Hetfield," and Morss wrote it with both letters as "Heatfield." Chestnut is written without the middle "t.". Young trees are called "saplins" without the customary "g" on the end. Many words are capitalized wherever they appear as well.

Today, it would be difficult, if not impossible, to locate any of the original boundary markers mentioned in the book. Among them are numbered stakes driven into the ground or white oak trees, which were then numbered. Other markers mentioned are chestnut, birch, and beech trees, or even bushes that were found on the properties in 1736.

Joseph Morss's grandson emigrated from England in 1664. Peter Morss (Morse) was a son of Anthony Morss of Wiltshire, England. Peter was at the Massachusetts Bay Colony in 1635, then went to Newberry, Rowley, and Long Island. He finally purchased lands in Elizabethtown in 1657. Peter Morss was Rahway's first settler, and his history is written in the archives in the town and church records of Elizabethtown, Woodbridge, and the vicinity. One of his descendants was Dr. Isaac Morss, Rahway's first physician.

On their plantation, in about 1700, the Morss family erected one of the earliest tidal gristmills in the area; it was the beginning of an industry that proved to be a successful undertaking through several generations of descendants. For decades, the mills and the farm were profitable. It is believed that British troops in a destructive march on Elizabeth in 1780 burned the mill, which stood where Morse's Mill Road now crosses the creek. Later rebuilt, the mill continued in operation until about 1870. The following stories are from a March 30, 1907 article in the *Elizabeth Daily Journal*, titled "Morss Farm Has New Owner" and subtitled "First Transfer of the Property Since 1657" and, "The Old Homestead Still Standing" also, "How Robert Morss Outwitted the British."

> One night while the British were fighting in our area, Mr. Morss heard some of the soldiers discussing means for removing the cattle early in the morning. So, late at night, he made his way downstairs to the

kitchen. He had to pass through the dining room where the soldiers were sleeping, stretched out on the floor. The sentinel asked him where he was going. He answered that his wife was not feeling well and he was going to make some tea. He passed on into the kitchen, made the tea, returning through the room, apparently going upstairs, but in reality slipped out the back door of the hall and went to the barn. He drove the cattle away to a place of safety. In the morning, the soldiers discovered the cattle were gone and inquired of Morss as to where they could be found, and he told them they had been driven to Elizabethtown during the night to the butcher.

A noteworthy transfer of property took place in Rahway at the office of Lawyer Leslie Lupton, on Thursday of last week when a deed was given by the owners of what is known as The Farm at Linden, to the Tremley Improvement Company.

This property had been continuously held by the Morss family since Peter Morss purchased it of the Indians in 1657, the descendants of Peter Morss living there, one generation after another, up to the time of the death of Anthony Morss, a few years ago. Among his papers were found many old deeds of historic value, especially the one originally given by the Indians. The old house, still standing, witnessed many stirring

MORSS FAMILY HOMESTEAD AND FARM. The property was located at Tremley Point from 1657 to 1907. (Courtesy UCHS.)

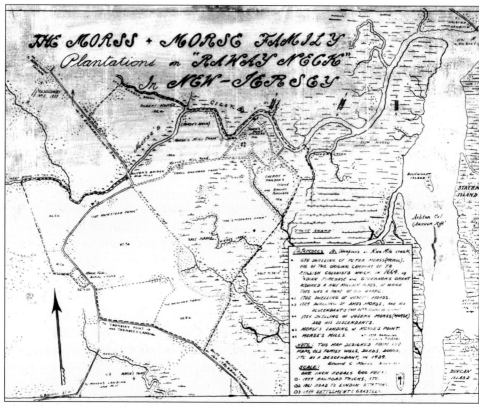

MORSS (MORSE) PLANTATION, 1938. The plantation was located in Linden in Tremley Point. Dr. Edward C. Morse, a Washington, D.C. physician, prepared and provided a drawn map that has been reprinted many times since 1938 for school children taking field trips to visit the gravestones to do "rubbings." (Courtesy UCHS.)

> events of 1776, being occupied repeatedly by British and American soldiers in their marches and countermarches [through] New Jersey from New York to Philadelphia.

The old homestead was still standing at the time of the sale of the property, and according to the article, "It has changed but little in appearance, except for natural decay, since the days of the Revolutionary War. It was a stopping place in their numerous raids through this section."

In October 1938, Dr. Edward C. Morse, a Washington, D.C. physician preparing a genealogy of the Morse family in America, "armed with what data was available, approached the area of what was once the plantation to find, to his surprise, a refinery." Dr. Morse was a family member of the eighth generation of the Morss clan, and his story of the 1938 excavation of the property in which three headstones were discovered appeared in the January 24, 1941 edition of the *Esso Refiner*. The story also provided a hand-drawn map that has been reprinted many times since for local schoolchildren on field trips to the Morss memorial stones, where the children do "rubbings."

In 1953, the Standard Oil Company of New Jersey, interested in preserving the historic landmarks of its refinery, erected a monument and set down the old stones as a memorial and a perpetual reminder of the older life of the land it now occupies. When the tank farm was built, all the graves were disturbed and destroyed. The Standard Oil Company's memorial tablet reads as follows:

> From this point north-easterly as far as the creek which bears their name, were the plantations of Peter Morss and many of his descendants for over 200 years. Peter and his brother Robert were among the earliest Europeans to settle this area known as Rahway Neck in the old bounds of Elizabeth- Towne. They were of the original company of eighty English colonists whose Indian Purchase and Governor's Grant in 1664 preceded the arrival of Captain Carteret and embraced half a million acres of this part of New Jersey.

First, Joseph Morss's stone shows he was born in 1709 and died in 1779. He was at one time Justice of the County Court of Quarter Sessions, and for many years, the surveyor for the Elizabethtown Associates. He headed the surveying party for two years, which laid out the vast area of over 25,000 acres west of Elizabethtown.

The next stone is that of Anne Winans Morss, who died in 1785 at 72. This is where the Winans family of Linden has one of their ancestors.

The final stone belongs to Susannah Trembly Morss, who died in 1801. The family name of Trembly is where our reference to the area of Linden as Tremley Point comes from. She is listed as the wife of Amos Morss, Joseph's brother, the proprietor of the western part of the original family plantation, whose large dwelling erected about 1750 was for many years the outstanding structure on Rahway Neck.

The Bayway refinery encompassed much of the land that formerly held prosperous tidewater plantations dating back to colonial days. A tidal creek, called Thompson's or Nine Mile Creek in early records and eventually Morse's Creek, separated the section into what were formerly called "Luke Watson's Neck" and "Rahway Neck." The property also included "Watson's Point," which was listed on maps of the 1700s.

The Winans family name also left an impact on New Jersey's geography, as there is a Winans Avenue in Cranford, Linden, and New Market, and a Winans Lane in Watchung. In the records, the name was spelled many ways: MaWynes, Waynes, Winons, Winnons, Wynons, Wynens, Wynans, Wynnings, and Winans.

Mariken, or Maria, Melyn came to New Netherlands in 1641 with her parents on the ship *Den Eyckenboom* (*The Oak Tree*). Her first husband, Claes Allertsen Paradys from Zutphen, was killed in the Indian Massacre on Staten Island in September 1655, and that same year, Maria went to New Haven, Connecticut with her parents and the other members of the family. She then married Matthias

Hitfield (Hatfield) in a double wedding ceremony on August 25, 1664. Her sister Susanna Melyn married John Winans, who was born in the Netherlands in 1640 to Jan Wyantz, on that same day. Maria's brother Jacob Melyn and his brothers-in-law, Matthias Hatfield, Humphrey Spinning, and John Winans, were among those residents of New Haven who were the original Associates who founded Elizabeth Town, New Jersey.

Susanna Melyn's husband John Winans was a weaver. According to Woodford Clayton's *History of Union and Middlesex Counties*, Winans did not have trouble finding work because, as Clayton puts it, weaving was "a handicraft in great request at that early day." Winans owned a house on a lot of 5 acres—Jacob Melyn and Humphrey Spinage as his immediate neighbors—and considerable property in other parts of Elizabethtown, the largest individual parcel consisting of 120 acres of upland terrain on "Peach Garden Brook." When Jacob Melyn moved to New York, Winans bought his house, lot, barn, orchard, and other property on February 8, 1678. John Winans and Susanna Melyn had nine children: John, Susannah, Elisbeth, Samuel, John, Johanna, Conrad, Jacob, and Isaac. John died in December 1694 in Elizabethtown.

It is believed that John Winans and Barnabas Wines, also known as Wynes and Winds, were part of the same family because their names were often spelled the same. Barnabas came to the area in 1665 and owned 164 acres. There is also record of a DeWitt C. Winans who died in 1694.

Moses Oliver Winans (1826–1900) and his wife, Sarah Elizabeth Hatfield Winans (1828–1911), were married in 1850 and had four children: Maline, Clarence Hatfield, Sarah Elizabeth, and Mary Louise. Moses was a mason and a farmer, and he made many land transactions in the area. He was also one of the original trustees of the Linden Methodist Church. Sarah Winans left the Presbyterian Church in 1851 to join the Methodist Church. Both are buried in the Evergreen Cemetery in Hillside. Their son Clarence Hatfield Winans (1854–1942) married Phoebe A. Wood (1856–1897) and fathered children Ada and Raymond.

Beginning in 1888, the C.H. Winans Company played a prominent role in building Linden's street system and was the first company to pave most of the streets in the town. Today, the company is located at 616 West First Avenue in Roselle. The company's first big job was constructing Edgar Road (Route 1) from Rahway to the Elizabeth line. From 1900 through the 1920s, Clarence H. Winans, as the company's first president, laid out and cut through Wood Avenue and dozens of other area streets. Through the years, the C.H. Winans Company has remained a family organization. In 1940, Raymond W. Winans succeeded his father as president, a position Raymond held until his death in 1944. Then, George W. Bauer, a founder of the firm and the husband of Ada Hatfield Winans (the daughter of founder C.H. Winans), served as president, and his son Raymond W. Bauer served as treasurer. George W. Bauer was also president of Linden Trust Company, which later became the Union County Trust Company. Another Winans home was 1215 North Wood Avenue.

WINANS FAMILY, 1865. This daguerreotype depicts the women members of the Winans family photographed in 1865. Daguerreotypes were photographs processed on metal plates. (Courtesy Ruth Etta Apalinski.)

The Rosedale Cemetery is situated on land that was once included among the farmlands of Moses Winans. His son Clarence legally had the land released from his father's will, and then bought out his brother Maline's piece. He had Maline remove all the buildings but the family homestead. Clarence then sold the parcel to a Mr. Smith who, in turn, sold it to the Rosedale Cemetery Association. The Winans homestead was then used as a guesthouse; it was razed in the 1970s.

Maline Winans, another son of Moses Winans, married Augusta, and the couple had two daughters: Cora and Etta Augusta. Etta Augusta Winans (1882–1965) married Fred McGillvray (1879–1967) on December 7, 1904, and they had children Fred, Sarah Mahar, Margaret Zimmer, and Ruth Fullerton, as well as 12 grandchildren. Fred McGillvray, a former Linden road commissioner and a member of the board of education, was one of four children, along with siblings William, Grace, and George. His family owned a dairy farm on St. George Avenue.

Among others descended from John Winans were Charles Clayton Winans of Linden, Mrs. Warren de Monti Morency of Westfield, Wilbur Roden of Linden, Mrs. John F. Edwards of Linden, and Ms. H. Perlee Bouton of Elizabeth.

The Roll family also played a prominent part in both the economic and civil life of Union County. Abraham Roll, the founder of the Roll family of Linden, settled in the Tremley section and his homestead and farmland remained in family ownership for many generations. But Abraham's son Isaac, born *c.* 1783, was the family member who accumulated the extensive land holdings that were, at one time, part of the family's heritage in Linden.

Smith S. Roll, the son of Isaac C. and Sarah Freeman Roll, married Arrena McPherson, and the couple had two daughters and one son: Mrs. Thomas H. Girtanner, Mrs. Joseph Loitsch, and Lloyd S. Roll. Smith S. Roll was a lifelong resident of Linden and a member of the Methodist Episcopal Church. During his residence, Smith witnessed the growth of his community from a township to a city.

Walter Roll was born on Stiles Street on July 7, 1898. His wife Madeline Banta was born in Elizabeth, but moved to Linden in 1910. She attended the "old barn" school before School One was established and graduated from Linden High when it was still part of the School One building. Madeline was a teacher in the Linden elementary schools for 23 years before retiring from Deerfield School Number 9. Her father was Herbert D. Banta, the Linden tax collector for many years. Walter Roll worked for the Union Carbide Company for 30 years before retiring.

ROLL FAMILY HOUSES OF THE 1800s. *The top picture shows the home of Isaac Roll, built in 1833, which stood on "Hancock Lane." The bottom picture is of the home of William Stone Roll at 2636 Tremley Point Road, built in 1856. Photographed in 1936 by Peter Mazonas. (Courtesy UCHS.)*

In an interview with the *Linden Leader* during the United States Bicentennial celebration in 1976, Roll paused to reflect while sitting in the living room of his then 50-year-old house, which was built by "old man Gesner either in 1905 or 1918, and was known to be the old Gesner house," at 821 Wood Avenue. Roll remembered the Gesners as one of the first families on Wood Avenue. By 1976, the neighborhood had changed dramatically since the swimming hole, hookey playing, and family picnic days of his boyhood.

> At that time, the large, curving branches of the trees formed an archway across the streets, which were fewer. When my father was president of the Board of Education, [he] built the old No.1 School in 1909, he was called a nut and people warned him there'd never be enough kids to fill it up. There were six students in my high school class and my sister, who was a year ahead of me, had seven in her class.

One of Walter Roll's most vivid reminiscences was of his grandfather living on lower Stiles Street in an old farmhouse until his death on June 20, 1912. Roll said that his grandfather, at the age of 87, was still arming and driving a yoke of oxen. Roll's father Walter Harrison Roll was born on lower Stiles Street on July 23, 1864.

He was an insurance broker and commuted to New York City. In the winter he wore boots and carried a lantern from his home on Stiles Street. At the station, he changed to shoes and left the boots and lantern there all day, to use when he returned in the evening. This is what most people did when commuting by train.

Roll also listed scenic memories of Linden:

> A great big hole in the ground where stores near the railroad are now. Meeker Wood, who had a big, black, square-cut beard and owned a lot of land. Fred Wood's cow pond. Johnny Penzak, the electrician, lived on the other side of the tracks where Curtis Street is now. Blancke Street was named after "old man Blancke" and the Blancke Farm ran past the creek up to Curtis Street's present location. Most residential estates were farms and only about 15 houses lined Wood Avenue.

Roll recalled, "Jim Lombardo was the truant officer but could never catch us kids when we played hookey." Walter Roll and his young friends gave the local swimming holes amusing names. Little Chicken and Big Chicken were for the smaller children, but Little Turkey and Big Turkey had deeper water and were just for the older boys. There was good salt water in those swimming holes until Standard Oil Company came along. "We had three or four swimming holes and used to go swimming on nice days—school or no school. One swimming hole was near Morris Avenue and the brush factory. Another was behind the Linden Laundry, and at the water hole at Curtis and Ainsworth Streets, which was for boys only, there was skinny-dipping."

Years ago, children would spend hours in the strawberry or blueberry patch and bring the fruit home to their mothers, who would make six or seven pies and give several to their neighbors. Farms were typical of much of Union County until after World War I, though there were still 200 farms and 53 dairy farms in Union County in the late 1950s. By the early 1970s, fewer than 90 farms of 10 acres or more were in existence, and only 3 dairy farms remained. By 1982, the county boasted a single milk distribution company, the Tuscan Dairy Company in Union Township, and all of their cows were gone.

The rapid growth of Rahway and Elizabeth brought the need for change in the form of local government of this area. By 1858, both municipalities had become cities. Linden, or Wheatsheaf as it was then called, continued to be partly in Rahway Township and partly in the city of Elizabeth. This complicated arrangement spurred the formation of Linden Township in 1861, and Rahway Township ceased to exist. The following men from the Linden area served in the government of Elizabethtown and then the Borough of Elizabeth, before Linden Township was created from Rahway and Elizabeth in 1861. This information is documented in the Weisbrodt-Newmark manuscript:

> Luke Watson, constable, commander of militia (commissioned lieutenant);
> Jonas Wood, deputy to the General Assembly (1693), justice of the peace (1710);
> Joseph Marsh, member of the General Assembly (1710), overseer of the highway;
> Samuel Melyen, overseer of the highway (1710);
> Samuel Winans, overseer of the highway (1712);
> Benjamin Spinning, constable (1714), overseer of the highway (1718);
> Stephen Crane, moderator (mayor) (1772, 1780);
> Amos Morse, assessor (1790), alderman (1798);
> Benjamin Winans, common council (1793, 1796);
> John Terrill, member of the General Assembly (1739, 1797);
> John Tooker, alderman (1794, 1799);
> Alston Marsh, common council (1796);
> Andrew Wilson, overseer of the poor (1801);
> Samuel Marsh, common council (1840);
> Daniel Marsh, assessor (1840);
> John Terrill, collector (1840);
> Ephraim Marsh, overseer of the poor (1840);
> David Mulford, director of the board of freeholders (1859, 1868), judge of the common pleas (1862, 1877), member of the General Assembly (1860, 1861);
> Elsten (Alston) Marsh, member of the General Assembly (1859, 1860);
> Ferdinand Blancke, member of the General Assembly (1870, 1875);
> David Naar, mayor of the borough of Elizabeth (1843).

Born on November 10, 1800 on the island of St. Thomas in the West Indies, David Naar (originally spelled Nahar) came to the United States when he was 15 years of age. He purchased a farm in Wheatsheaf in 1835. In addition to serving as mayor of the Borough of Elizabeth, Naar held other civil offices, as well. He was a judge of the Court of Pleas for Essex County (1843), a delegate to the Constitution Convention of 1844, United States consul to St. Thomas, recorder of the Borough and a member of Borough Council (1848–1851), clerk of the General Assembly (1851 and 1852), and, finally, state treasurer in 1865. Naar moved to Trenton in 1853, when he purchased the *American*, a newspaper that became the leading Democratic journal of New Jersey. David Naar died on February 24, 1880. He was the first Jewish mayor in the United States.

In addition, the following men of the Linden area served in the Township of Rahway, before Linden Township was created from Rahway and Elizabeth. This information is located on page 133 of the Weisbrodt-Newmark manuscript:

> James Marsh, overseer of highway (1804); overseer of the poor (1804, 1805);
> Ralph Marsh, overseer of highway (1804), township committee (1804);
> Amos Morse, judge of election (1804), assessor (1805);
> Anthony Morse, freeholder (1804, 1805), township committee (1804);

THE EVIA RESIDENCE. The home is the oldest building in Linden and was originally built in the 1700s. It is located at 417 South Wood Avenue. (Courtesy UCHS.)

John Tucker, commissioner of appeals (1804), township committee
  chairman (met at Wheatsheaf), chairman 1805, pound keeper 1804;

Anthony Winans, overseer of highway (1804);

Samuel Winans, collector (1804), overseer of the poor (1804, 1810),
  commissioner of appeals (1805), township committee (1807);

Isaac O. Winans, township committee (1807);

William Shotwell, overseer of roads (1809);

Jacob Terril, overseer of roads (1809);

Joseph Garthwaite, overseer of roads (1809);

Stephen Winans, overseer of roads (1809);

John E. Wood, overseer of roads (1809), constable (1816);

Abraham Marsh, farmer of the poor (1810);

William Wood, overseer of roads (1810);

David Wood, overseer of roads (1813);

Charles Tucker, overseer of roads (1813);

Elihu Marsh, overseer of roads (1813);

Sam Trembley, overseer of roads (1813);

Amos Tucker, overseer of roads (1813);

Johnathan Tremley, overseer of roads (1813, 1829);

Gideon Tucker, township committee (1817);

Aaron Shotwell, township committee (1817 and 1824).

*JOHN POTTER WINANS FAMILY, c. 1865. John Potter Winans and his family are pictured
here at the Linden homestead. (Courtesy Apalinski family.)*

3. WHEATSHEAF

Elizabethtown included a number of small villages that are important to the history of Linden. Among these were Wheatsheaf, Tremley, Upper Rahway, and Greater Elizabeth. Although the name is deceiving, the area of Greater Elizabeth is now the Eighth Ward of Linden.

In the colonial era, each village area was required to have either a tavern or an inn for the benefit of travelers and neighborhood residents. The tavern was used as a public building where elections and political meetings took place and were often used as meeting places by the military during the Revolution.

The Wheatsheaf Tavern is one of three taverns shown on the "Elizabeth-Towne" map made by Robert Erskine, the official cartographer to General George Washington, in 1777. Thomas Gordon, writing about the community that surrounded the Wheatsheaf Tavern in his *Gazetteer of New Jersey* (1834), reported, "It is a small village on the line separating Rahway from Elizabeth Town, eight miles S.W. from Newark, and half way between Elizabethtown and Bridgetown (a 'village' of Rahway), three miles from either; it contains a tavern, from whose sign it has its name; a store and eight or ten dwellings." It was located at what would now be the intersection of Roselle Street at St. Georges Avenue.

St. Georges Avenue is one of the oldest major roads in New Jersey and is known today as State Highway 27. Formerly a unit of the Lincoln Highway, which was at one time considered the transcontinental highway of the United States, St. Georges Avenue was called Queen Anne's Highway during the reign of Queen Anne (1865–1714). It extended from Perth Amboy to Elizabeth Town Point and onward to Newark by taking in Broad Street as a continuation of the roadway. When King George came into power in England, the roadway was extended to Jersey City and was renamed the King's Highway. St. Georges Avenue was first laid out to be six rods (99 feet) wide and was a dirt road until 1888, when macadam pavement was laid down the center. It remained this way until 1923 when the roadway was paved with asphalt and concrete. During the Revolution, the highway became known as the Post Road and was one of the principal military roads. After the Revolutionary War, the name was again changed, this time to the Old Country Road. When Rahway became a city, the route's name was again changed to St. Georges Avenue. Traveling from Trenton, George Washington rode through Linden on St. Georges Avenue on the journey to his inauguration. When he reached Elizabeth Port, he then traveled by boat to New York City. General Lafayette traveled down St. Georges Avenue to Rahway in August 1824 and also passed through Linden with much festivity.

The Wheatsheaf Tavern was constructed as far back as 1745, and consisted of a two-and-a-half story main section and a one-and-a-half-story wing. The first landlord of the inn was Henry Broadwell. At that time, it was known as the George Tavern, after King George.

Broadwell remained landlord until 1764, when he rented the house to Soverign Sybrant, who tried to set up a stagecoach service there. It was to be "a genteel stage wagon" that was to set out from Philadelphia on Monday and get to Trenton the same day. Sybrant's venture, however, soon failed.

The next landlord, a Mr. Wilkinson, seems to have been the first to use the name Wheatsheaf. Records indicate that John Chetwood and John Blanchard, trustees of the estate of Jonathan Hampton of Elizabeth Town, offered the old tavern for sale in 1783. Isaac Marsh conducted the inn between 1790 and 1801, and his widow Rhoda ran it for two more years. Jonas Cooper owned the inn from 1804 to 1810.

An advertisement in the February 20, 1837 edition of the *Elizabeth Journal* describes the tavern as follows: "Large and commodious house and grocery store, outhouses, excellent garden, an acre and 1/4 of land. Well with very good water and a number of fine fruit trees on premises. It is equidistant from Rahway and Elizabeth."

John Yates was the next landlord from 1837 to 1843, followed by Oliver Halsey from 1844 to 1849. In 1861, the inn was owned by John B. Day. It was here that Linden Township had its first annual town meeting as enacted by the state legislature.

In 1912, the old Wheatsheaf was purchased by Christian Winters. The family consisted of wife Lauraetta and children Conrad, Christan, Anna, Amira, and Laura. Anna and Laura recently sent correspondence to the Union County Historical Society. In it, they remembered the following:

> The building was moved in 1919, when an extension of Chestnut Street was proposed. The original, two-and-a-half-story section was moved just far enough to be out of the way, about 100 feet from its original location. It was moved a few hundred feet along Wheatsheaf Road. Laura Winters remembered that her dad was compensated $200.00, with most being spent on the move. The Old School which became the Recreation Hall was separated and moved a short distance behind the inn building and was converted into a house for her sister Anna Colohan who had married in 1916. Christian and Lauraetta opened a corner of the Wheatsheaf as a country store selling bread, candy, tobacco, hardware and gasoline. This fuel was pumped by hand into a storage tank at the top of the pump, then gravity delivered it to the customer.

There were also other businesses around the area when the Wheatsheaf was first built. In 1682, William Broadwell was by trade a cordwainer and had a tannery in the area.

THE WHEATSHEAF INN, 1937. The inn was moved to clear a way for Chestnut Street to be continued through to St. Georges Avenue. It is now the only house located on Wheatsheaf Road (next to the gas station at the corner of St. Georges Avenue). (Courtesy UCHS.)

4. TREMLEY

The village of Tremley (spelled also as Trembley and Trembly in the past) was first settled by the families of the earliest Elizabeth Town colonists. The area takes its name from the French Huguenot Jean Traubles, whose name has been anglicized in the area and in succeeding generations of his family over time.

A number of important roadways ran through the area and helped contribute to the community's growth and prosperity. Both the Lower Road (to Rahway) of today and Tremley Point Road are pre–Revolutionary War thoroughfares, the latter leading to Rahway Neck (later Tremley Point). Along the Lower Road, one can see the grave markers of members of the Morse family at the point at which Lower Road becomes Stiles Street. Stiles Street, which can be found on the 1862 map of Linden, is the only street to cut across the breadth of Linden and connect with Tremley Point Road; however, Morses Mill Road (and the Lower Road to Rahway) also connected at the old Tremley Point Road, which was one of the few main thoroughfares in the township of Linden. In a deed dated September 6, 1817, conveying a parcel of land from Daniel and Rebecca Caddington to Elias Tooker, the land is described as being bounded by a "two rod Road called the Forty Acre Road." It was used in the seventeenth century. Marshes Dock Road is also classified among the old roads in Linden, and Wood Avenue is shown on the 1862 map, though a great deal shorter than it is today. In 1862, Wood Avenue stretched from what is today Blancke Street to approximately 15th Street, but it was extended to St. Georges Avenue in 1868 and to Morses Mill Road in 1901.

One of the first sawmills in the area was Marsh Mill, built by John Marsh on the south side of the Rahway River. The first permit for a dam was issued to John Marsh and dated January 26, 1683, but it was also necessary for Marsh to secure a permit from Elizabeth Town. The following gives the terms imposed by this permission:

> A meeting of ye Inhabitants of Elizabethtown, June 25, 1683: Voted that John Marsh have Liberty and Consent from ye towne so far as they are Concerned to get Timber to saw at his Saw-mill upon Land not Surveyed lying upon Rahway River or ye branches or elsewhere far as he shall have occasion to fetch timber for above mill.

Another permit was granted to John Marsh on December 19, 1684 because he was also interested in the milling of grain. His mill was later sold to Stephen Van Courtlandt, and then to William Donaldson in 1733. In 1739, Donaldson sold his interest to Samuel Marsh and Joseph Meyer. The property remained in the Marsh family until 1826, when it was bought by Lufbery and Vail, later Ayres and Lufbery. The mill was run by waterpower until the milldams were removed in 1855. These dams were abolished through an act of the legislature after the action was put to a vote in an 1853 public meeting in Rahway. The issue was raised by area doctors who were concerned by the malarial fevers that were produced by the stagnant waters. The dams removed were owned by Jesse C. Hardenberg; Ayres, Williams and Lufbery; Henry B. Shotwell; and Isaac Jones. Waterpower was then replaced by steam for manufacturing purposes, a development that led to increased prosperity.

Located on the bend of the Rahway River at Tremley Point, Densler's Grove was a popular inn, which was owned and managed by Christopher Densler. It was patronized, to a great extent, by seamen. For instance, Jacob Marsh (d. 1832) and his younger brother Thomas (d. 1856) owned a large vessel, *Sarah Francis* (named after a younger sister), that was used to transport bricks from the pits along the Rahway River to New York and elsewhere; the Marsh brothers docked at Densler's. Many clambakes (of a political nature) were held at Densler's Grove in the 1880s, and the inn was also the site of picnic parties and swimming excursions.

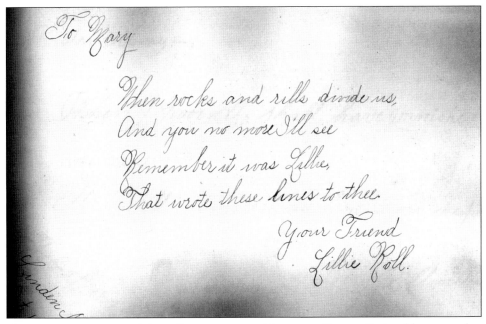

AUTOGRAPH BOOK OF MARY BILLWILLER OF TREMLEY POINT. Scripted by none other than Lillie Roll in 1894, this is a beautiful hand-tooled leather autograph book. Its first entries are dated from 1884. It traces friends of Mary Billwiller through 1907. (Courtesy L. Yeats.)

GENERAL ANILINE CORPORATION. *The site is located in the Tremley industrial area. (Courtesy UCHS.)*

With the exception of a few farms, this area remained largely undeveloped for more than 200 years. However, due to its excellent location for shipping, the area attracted two industries around 1870: Russell Coe's bone and acid works and the S.S. Fales Chemical Works. Other pioneer Linden industries around the turn of the nineteenth century included the General W.J. Bush Company; the Linden Tanning Company; the John Stephens Company, which manufactured trolleys; the Mountain Copper Company, smelters; Swan, Finch, and Company, oil refiners; and Warner Asphalt Company.

In 1898, the township committee rushed the construction of the Shore Road, as large tankers began to dock at the Linden waterfront bringing in supplies, and freight cars, trucks, and pipelines soon carried away finished products. Linden's proximity to New York (18 miles) and Newark (12 miles) gave it all the advantages of a great metropolitan area, and the road was crucial to the growth of local industries.

The Standard Chemical Works moved to Tremley Point in Linden in 1880, and in 1888, Thomas Grasselli bought Standard Chemical Works and established the Grasselli Chemical Company of Cleveland, which manufactured sulfuric acid. The site was designed to serve New Jersey's rapidly growing oil industry. The area was only a few feet above the high-water mark and could be reached only by boat or over a plank walk. Water was brought to the plant by earthen jugs or by wooden canal boats from Elizabethport. In winter, the cost of getting boats through the ice-filled Staten Island Sound was sometimes as great as the worth of their cargos.

The West Works of Grasselli was purchased by General Aniline in 1915. The company's name was changed from Grasselli Chemical Company to Grasselli Dyestuffs Company and, in 1928, to General Aniline Works, Inc. to indicate the transition to full ownership by the German manufacturers. The name was changed again in 1939 to the General Aniline and Film Corporation.

Occupying 51 buildings set on more than 100,000 piles, and covering 118 acres, the plant of the East Works of Grasselli was virtually a "city on stilts." The Grasselli Chemical Company also constructed barracks in the area during World War I and, by 1920, had begun building permanent workers' housing in the Tremley Point district. The occupants of these Grasselli-built homes were given a 99-year lease; however, when Du Pont purchased the company in 1942, it authorized the Fedor Real Estate Agency to sell the houses. Other chemical products were soon added to the product line of the newly acquired company, a move that helped to relieve the country's dependence on European sources for the basic chemicals needed for expansion and growth. Du Pont also donated the land for Memorial Park.

The Tremley Point district is both the southernmost and the easternmost residential neighborhood in Linden. This small, isolated neighborhood is located among fields of oil tanks east of Linden Airport and west of the New Jersey Turnpike. Most of the district lies in the angle formed by the juncture of the Lower Road to Rahway and Tremley Point Road. Memorial Park, north of Tremley Point Road, completes the district. Throughout the district, modest homes were placed close to the street on small lots. The district also includes two churches and a small business section.

Development in the Tremley Point district was initiated when John Fedor laid out streets with small building lots for workers' housing. Fedor, who began his career in real estate in 1903 with the Realty Trust Company of New York, organized the Realty Estates of Linden in 1907 and began developing areas on both the west and east sides of Edgar Road. In 1916, after forming the John Fedor Realty Company at 530 South Wood Avenue in Linden, he continued development of the area east of Edgar Road, including the tract now known as Tremley Point. The streets of the eastern portion of the community bear Fedor family names, such as Irene, Walter, and Arthur. Fedor was able to visualize great use of Linden for both industry and development. He was instrumental in helping Grasselli locate to the area, and the Grasselli Company was instrumental in rounding out the community by constructing the houses west of Main Street and by providing the district with a community center (now Monsignor Komar Hall).

The Tremley Point community continued to grow, as did the refineries and chemical works. Soon, the village was bordered on three sides by fields of large tanks, mainly those of Standard Oil Company. The residents developed a cohesive community, and these prewar inhabitants were characterized by longtime residents as "jolly people" who loved to dance and sing. At that time, there was a covered platform at the end of Irene Street where dances were held, and there were several social clubs where Slovak and Scotch-Irish residents relaxed after a day's work. After World War II, some of the unity was lost as children of the original residents began to move to other places. However, the effect of the community spirit generated by the Tremley Point district can still be felt today.

The older houses, dating from the early 1900s, are located east of Main Street. Many have hipped roofs; others have gabled roofs and have been placed with the gable end to the street. Some are two-family houses. This section also contains a small commercial district on Tremley Point Road. The focal point of the district is Monsignor Komar Hall, a rambling Tudor building that faces the green at the corner of Main Street.

The decision of the Standard Oil Company (predecessor to the Esso Standard Oil Co., Exxon, and Tosco) to locate one of its largest refineries in Linden was the turning point of the city from a farming and rural area to what has become one of the most important industrial communities in the state. The area occupied by the Bayway Refinery was once a series of pastures and fields on both sides of Morse's Mill Creek. The refinery's history began on January 18, 1908, with the laying of the cornerstone for the machine shop. Work on the plant started in the fall of 1907, and the construction of temporary office buildings, begun on October 15, was completed by December 1 of that year. Most of the construction effort during that fall, however, was devoted to the clearing and grading of land. Five batteries of pipe stills and treating facilities constituted the nucleus of the original refinery, which had an initial capacity of 10,000 barrels a day.

STANDARD OIL COMPANY. *This photograph shows the laying of the cornerstone at Machine Shop No. 2 at the Standard Oil Company of New Jersey site in Linden on January 18, 1908. (Courtesy UCHS.)*

5. LINDEN TOWNSHIP

The mid-1800s were a time of changing boundaries. Union County separated from Essex County in 1857, and the township of Rahway was formed in 1858. What is now the city of Linden was then mostly Rahway, partly Elizabeth, and a small piece of Union. On March 4, 1861, an act of the state legislature created the township of Linden, which, at that time, had a population of 1,146. The area included present-day Roselle, Winfield Park, and a small portion of Cranford, in addition to present-day Linden. In 1871, there were about 40 homes in the township.

With the creation of the new township came the necessity of establishing a government and civic services. In Linden, early town meetings were held annually at the Wheatsheaf Tavern, and at these meetings, qualified voters would elect five men to represent them. This committee served as the governing force of the township, and each member was elected to a one-year term. Other township officials included a clerk, a collector, and an assessor. The number of committee members varied throughout the years. Between 1861 and 1869, there were five members; between 1870 and 1894, there were eight (two from each road district).

At a March 12, 1897 public meeting held at what was then known as the Petros Hotel (also called the Linden Hotel and Zuckers Hotel), a resolution authorized the building of the town hall at a cost not to exceed $1,500. The citizens approved of the plan in a special election.

The first public building erected in the township of Linden was a town hall, located on the site now occupied by the Engine Company No. 1 firehouse on the southeast corner of Morris and Wood Avenues. A plot of land (50 by 168 feet) was bought from C.H. Winans in 1898, and the contract to build was given to Charles A. Long of Rahway for $1,447. A two-story, wood-frame structure was built and served as Linden's town hall until 1916. It was then sold and moved across South Wood Avenue; it has since been renovated into a family residence located at 124 South Wood Avenue.

The second municipal building to be erected in and by Linden Township was another town hall, which was constructed in 1911 on a slight rise, looking up Wood Avenue toward the railroad station. The building's architect was Louis Quien Jr. The structure boasts the neoclassical style. Two other examples of the neoclassical architectural style in Linden were the Linden Trust Company, located at 201 North Wood Avenue, and Linden City Hall, located at 301 North Wood Avenue. Listed on the Union County Cultural and Heritage Programs Advisory Board (UCCHPAB) Historical Survey of 1981, the first phase of the Union County's Sites Inventory was initiated in 1980 by the UCCHPAB under a matching grant from the Department of Environmental Protection, the Bureau of Parks and Forestry, and the Office of Historic Preservation. The town hall today houses the Department of Recreation, Community Service, and Public Property.

Of special historical significance, Thomas Alva Edison conducted a lighting experiment in the village of Roselle (earlier known as Mulford) while it was still part of Linden Township. The area was chosen because it did not have gas lighting, and at the time, it was feared that gas and electricity should not be mixed. Edison set out to prove that a town could be lighted by electricity from a single generating station, in this case, one located at the northeast corner of Locust Street and West First Avenue. The generator was started on January 19, 1883, and it sent power through overhead wires strung on poles to a store, railroad station, about 40 houses, and streetlights. In April of that year, the First Presbyterian Church of Roselle was the first church in the world to be lighted when a 30-bulb electrolier—which can still be seen today—was installed inside.

On November 2, 1889, the Central Electric Company of New York obtained permission to erect poles in the township of Linden, after obtaining the property owners' approval for the proposed line. After the incorporation of the borough of Roselle in 1894, the first electric lights in the township were situated on St. Georges Avenue and on Wood Avenue, and were turned on December 14, 1899. The township was liable for the expense of ten lights on St. Georges Avenue and three on Wood Avenue. By April 9, 1902, there were 100 electric lamps in use throughout the township. As the years passed, the number of lights increased proportionally with the new construction. Prior to the advent of electricity, streets in the area were illuminated with gas lamps that were maintained by a lamplighter employed by the township.

Immediately after the incorporation of the township of Linden on March 4, 1861, residents wanted a post office that would be separate from Rahway and Elizabeth. On May 7, 1866, a post office was finally established in the township, and John Clay Jr. became the first postmaster. Christopher Boyne succeeded him on July 9, 1867, and served until March 16, 1868, when he was succeeded by Meeker Wood. Other early postmasters included F.C. Millett, Charles T. Warren, William T. Clark, Henry W. Gesner, William A. Stone Jr., David O. Hilliard, and William K. Schenk. The only woman to serve as postmaster in Linden was Sadie M. Wood, who was appointed on September 6, 1911 and served until Michael T. Quinn was appointed on March 1, 1915. Quinn served only a few months, and Alexander R. Corbet took over on May 13, 1915. Sadie M. Wood then became acting postmaster for a second time on October 1, 1917 and Postmistress in 1918.

In 1920, the post office and its carrier service were in danger of being removed from Linden when postal authorities seriously considered transferring the office to Elizabeth and reestablishing rural free delivery service in Linden. (At the time, some

TOWNSHIP OF LINDEN DOCUMENT OF INCORPORATION. On March 4, 1861, an act of state legislature created Linden Township. (Courtesy Richard Koziol.)

districts were already being served by the rural carrier route conducted by Elizabeth.) The Linden community sought to find a suitable building in which to continue to conduct post office business, and Postmistress Wood fought to keep the post office in Linden open. By 1921, the post office was housed in the borough hall.

The first building to be constructed as a post office was erected in October 1927 on Elizabeth Avenue, and the Linden post office was given first-class status on July 1, 1934, making Linden eligible for a government-constructed building. Samuel Lamont Jr. became postmaster on November 15, 1920; he was followed by Lorenzo S. Spates on January 30, 1922 and Herbert Schulhaffer on March 19, 1934. Linden also maintained another post office, housed in the Grasselli depot of the Central Railroad of New Jersey. At the time, the post office served only the industries on the waterfront, including Warner-Quinlan, American Cyanamid, and Sinclair Oil. Today the main office is on North Wood Avenue and was built in 1938, the Grasselli Station is located at the corner of South Wood Avenue and West Tenth Street, and Station A is located on St. George's Avenue.

The first telephones in Linden were installed in 1902, and the first telephone directory to include Linden was published by the New York and New Jersey Telephone Company on May 10, 1903. There were 19 Linden telephone subscribers in this first book. One of Linden's earlier industries, W.J. Bush

JAMES T. BERSEY. Bersey accomplished a lot of good for Linden. These badges denote a few of his roles: Linden Township Fire Department, Linden Township Volunteer Fire Department, City of Linden Fire Department Chief, and Linden councilman. (Courtesy Robert Bersey.)

Company, located on West Stimpson Avenue, was anxious to establish a telephone connection with its New York office, according to the *Elizabeth Daily Journal* in an anniversary newspaper.

In November 1908, the township committee addressed the appointment of policemen by ordinance to protect the citizens of the township. Prior to that time, constables were elected to the position for a term of one year. Three patrolmen were appointed to begin work on January 1, 1909: Frank Novella, Frederick Covery, and Arnold Hergenhan. The police department assumed its present form on May 5, 1919. At that time, the force included Captain Hickey (who went on to become chief) and Lieutenant Arnold Hergenhan.

The members of the Linden Township Fire Department were all volunteers, and the department included the following companies: U.S. Grant Volunteer Hose Company, the George Washington Volunteer Hose Company, the Central Volunteer Hose Company, the Lincoln Volunteer Hose Company (Tremley), and the Linden Hill Volunteer Hose Company.

The township of Linden contributed to the support of the volunteer organizations by funding supplies for the fire departments and, in time, by paying for water from the Elizabethtown Water Company to hook up the fire hydrants as they were constructed. Volunteers erected four small firehouses in the township, which the city later acquired title to. The authorization of the first municipal firehouse came in 1915, and the cornerstone of this firehouse was laid on June 10, 1916.

The president of the first fire company was James T. Bersey, who became chief in 1923. Bersey was one of the early settlers in the Greater Elizabeth area of Linden, now known as the Eighth Ward. The area was known as "Greater Elizabeth" because the Elizabeth railroad station was the nearest one to the area and early real estate developers named it that so people coming out to see the land would get off at the right station. Bersey was born in Bayonne and first came to the area in 1899. He built a house on Gilchrest Avenue and remembered that at that time there were only about seven families in the section and Standard Oil Company had not yet arrived Linden.

Bersey was proud of the role he played in the amalgamation of the borough and township. At the time of the merger, a majority of the people in Greater Elizabeth were against it, most of them preferring to join the City of Elizabeth when Linden Township merged with the Borough of Linden in 1925 to create the city. Bersey was instrumental in bringing the Greater Elizabeth area into the merger, and he was also instrumental in getting Grier Avenue put through. Besides being one of Linden's early fire chiefs, Bersey was the first councilman from the Eighth Ward, serving from 1925 until 1928. His family still owns the fire chief's badge of office, which Bersey once wore, as well as badges from his other offices in Linden.

The volunteer companies remained in existence until 1925, when the newly formed city abolished them. The appointment of Elmer Glover as fire engine driver, in 1925, marked the beginning of the paid fire department. Glover was not only paid but also provided with living accommodations. He went on to become the deputy fire chief of the city.

Wells were the main source of water for the township. Permission was granted for the laying of water pipes in the following roadways in 1892: Stiles, Henry,

LINDEN FIRE DEPARTMENT. The first fully-paid fire department was housed at the No. 1 house located on Wood Avenue at Morris Avenue. Standing in front of the 1916 American La France Pumper are, left to right, Lieutenant William Niemek, William Lindsay, and Edward Schekler. With the 1926 American La France Ladder Truck are, left to right, Leo Ratel, Anthony Schreck, Captain Elmer Glover, Michael Bancey, William Krosnowsky, Chief Frank Miler, Albert Wilke, and Ernest Mahar. (Courtesy LFD, Larry Lukenda.)

Blancke, and Price Streets, and Wood, Elizabeth, Washington, and Linden Avenues. However, this franchise to the Linden Water Company was cancelled in 1894. Another franchise was granted to the Linden Water Company in 1894, and that franchise was revoked in 1896. Finally, the Elizabethtown Water Company arrived and succeeded in holding their franchise.

The need for sewers was made apparent to the township committee as early as June 5, 1880. Sewerage has always been a problem for the township of Linden; had the sewerage dispute between what is now Roselle and the rest of Linden Township been settled, the separation of Roselle as a borough probably would not have been achieved at that time. At the March 6, 1893 meeting of the township committee, permission was granted to the Roselle Sewerage Company to lay pipes. On December 10, 1894, final permission for the construction of the sewer system was granted to the Roselle Company, after the withdrawal of the borough of Roselle from the township. At that time, permission was also given to Cranford, a neighboring New Jersey city, to run a sewerage pipe through Linden upon the acceptance of certain conditions. Linden had nothing to do with the actual construction of the sewer by Roselle.

In 1905, civil engineer Jacob L. Bauer was employed by the township and the borough of Linden to survey and estimate the cost of a sewer. After some controversy, the joint borough-township construction of a sewer was authorized in 1907 and work on the project began. The total cost of construction was $52,441, of which the township paid 45 percent and the borough paid 55 percent. Three sewer commissioners were appointed on June 17, 1912—Edmund Mayes, Frank R. Anderson, and Walter C. Bauer—to assess the land adjoining the sewer. The Greater Elizabeth area and St. Georges section of Linden were served by a joint sewer with Roselle.

The collection and disposal of garbage was also a big problem for both the township and the borough, and it may be said that the institution of this service was an indicator of the awakening of civic consciousness. Garbage was collected in the township of Linden sporadically in the years prior to December 22, 1920. On that date, an ordinance was passed calling for the collection of garbage by municipal means under the supervision of the "Overseer of Roads." Today, the collection of garbage is still a municipal function in the City of Linden.

The township of Linden also became aware of the need for community parks in 1923. On October 8, 1923, an ordinance was passed that proposed the buying of land at Wood Avenue and Edgar Road from Coloman Danninger and John Fedor, and on December 1, 1924, an ordinance was passed to give the care, custody, and control of the park property to the Union County Park Commission. On December 30, the commission accepted these proposals, and the park was later named after John Russell Wheeler, the first soldier from Linden to die in World War I.

Linden Township also boasted a horse racetrack, built in 1889. The track did good business and drew large crowds. Legislation was passed legalizing both horseracing and the betting of money on the races. The large sum of money paid

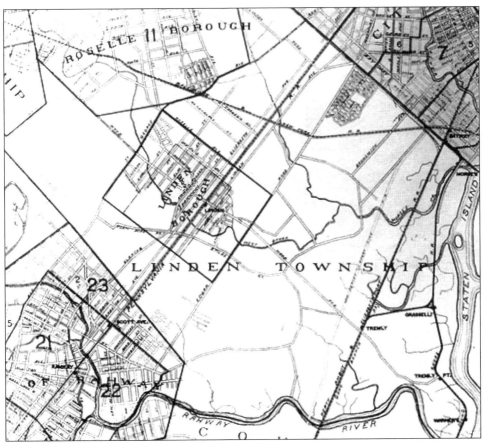

LINDEN TOWNSHIP AND LINDEN BOROUGH MAP, 1906. This map is from the Union County Atlas. (Courtesy UCHS.)

in the form of taxes to the state from these racetracks was likely a determining factor in the legalization. The Newmark-Weisbrodt WPA manuscript *The History of Linden*, reads as follows:

> In 1890, the assessment on the Linden Park Blood Horse Association was increased by $25,000; this was likely a significant increase, as it was fiercely contested. Two months later, the county freeholders granted the Linden Blood Horse Association a license to race horses. This action, however, was strongly protested by the township committee, but after 3 months of the dispute, the township issued a license to the racetrack for five years. The township was to receive $5,000 per year for five years from the track. The first $5,000 received by the township from the association was offered to the Roselle Sewer Company. (The township finally realized that the problem of sewerage in the Roselle area was being neglected.)

DOGTRACK ROUTE #25. This was also the site of a horsetrack during the early 1900s. Park Avenue is on the right side. Towards the upper right of the image is the site of picnic grounds that were used by the Knights of Columbus. The building we know today as Columbia Hall was created from the existing site in this image. (Courtesy L. Yeats.)

Still upset over the sewerage issue, the Roselle Sewer Company refused the money.

The facility, which measured 1.25 miles around, operated at the turn of the century as the Trenton Blueblood Racing Association, and President James Garfield was often an interested spectator at the Linden races. Track patrons would sometimes ride the train to Linden from New York City, debarking for a short walk to the track. The Pennsylvania Railroad tracks ran directly past the horse track, just north of Linden Avenue. After the track closed, the land stayed vacant for about 25 years.

Racing started early in the Province of New Jersey, as Colonel Lewis Morris wrote about it in his memorial concerning the state of religion in the Jerseys in 1700. In an effort to restrict the abuse of horse racing in the colony and to prevent lotteries, card playing, dicing, and other gambling for money, an act was passed by the Assembly in 1748 prohibiting horseracing except at fairs and on the first working days after Christmas, Easter, and Whitsuntide. However, it was lawful for any "Body Politick" or "Body Corporate" in the Province to cause, on certain fair days, to be offered any piece of plate or any sum of money not exceeding a value of £25 "to be run, paced, or trotted or otherwise rode for, by two or more horses, as they shall think fit." The Act of 1748 having failed to curtail an excess of racing, another act passed in 1761 abolished all races except those under special permission from the magistrate. Because of the need to improve the breed of horses, authority was given to three magistrates to legalize a race at any time by giving written permission, provided they attended in person in order to prevent wagers, drunkenness, and other disorderly conduct.

Just across Edgar Road from the racetrack, Bernard "Brownie" Plungis, along with his brothers George, Henry Sr., and Eddie Sr., operated the East Edgar Road Garage during the early 1920s. The brothers were adept at such diverse modes of transportation as the early airplane, power racing boats, midget racing cars, and iceboats. When Brownie's brother George flew his Waco Nine bi-plane into the town, he often touched down in the infield of the abandoned racetrack across from the garage. Brownie was only a young boy when the track was shut down but he remembered the final event. "The last race at the track was a steeple chase in 1908," he said.

In the southwest corner of the track grounds was an old farmhouse where Plungis had attended school as a boy. "We had two teachers and I remember an orchard by the school from which we would pick apples. Eventually, the school burned down and they brought a portable four-room school to the spot."

Standard Oil of New Jersey owned the property that the racetrack occupied, as well as the land extending to the Elizabeth city line, and the company later installed oil-storage tanks on one end of the abandoned track. When the wooden grandstand at the track burned to the ground in 1905, the jockey houses on the site were purchased as residences for townspeople in what is now Linden's Eighth Ward.

Some 25 years later, the Sims family of Elizabeth bought the site and constructed a new grandstand at the east end of the former thoroughbred track. The facility then catered to greyhound racing, and the Zupkis family dogs thrilled the betting crowds.

It was during the years between the departure of the thoroughbreds and the arrival of the dogs that George Plungis, flying his airplane that could reach speeds of 80 miles per hour, became a familiar sight landing in the infield. George purchased the plane from its original owner, a member of the first *Daily News* aerial photography team, and flew the two-seater from Roosevelt, Long Island, to its new home at South Plainfield's Hadley Field.

The 1920s saw many changes in the lifestyle of the citizens of Linden. As industry grew, farms began to decline, though many struggled to hold on until the 1950s. One of the largest, Lampert's farm, was dissolved in 1972, after having been reduced to a simple dairy store. But along with this decline came a new crisis, Prohibition. St. Georges Avenue, an important road during the Revolutionary War, played a significant role in Prohibition between 1920 and 1933 as bootleggers transported alcohol along the route to various drop points. Many speakeasy establishments in this area were served via St. Georges Avenue.

6. The Borough of Linden

The incorporation of the borough of Linden differed from the incorporation of the township. The township was formed by an enactment of the state legislature, while the borough was formed by a court order following the dictates of a general election.

Records at the Union County Courthouse reveal some of the reasons for the formation of the borough. Residents who wanted to form a separate community from the township of Linden sought well-lit roads and sidewalks, if only to walk or ride to the railroad station. Those in the farming district, however, were opposed to such changes. As owners of large parcels of land, they faced a substantial increase in taxes for the improvements. Thus, a petition for an election to form the borough of Linden as a new municipality was begun. The borough would become one of the few municipalities in the nation completely surrounded by another political division, with the township encompassing it like a doughnut.

The borough of Linden was incorporated on March 28, 1882. The statement of the result of an election held in the township of Linden, from the Newmark-Weisbrodt manuscript, follows:

> . . . to decide the will of the People for or against the establishment of a Borough Commission to be known as the Borough Committee of Linden, New Jersey, and to be bounded as follows: commencing at a point in the middle of the block between Linden and Morris Avenues, one hundred feet south of Maple Avenue extending thence through the middle of said block to a point one hundred feet south of Franklin Avenue, northwest parallel with Franklin Avenue to a point one hundred feet west of Curtis Street, thence northeast a line running parallel with Curtis Street to a point hundred feet south of Maple Avenue thence parallel with Wood Avenue to the place of beginning. The whole number on the Poll List is thirty-nine (39). The whole number of ballots rejected is none.
>
> For Borough Commission received thirty (30).
> Against Borough Commission received nine (9).

The borough of Linden was organized under a commission form of government. There were six members on the commission, or council, by 1896, after which time this number remained constant for the life of the borough. The commissioners chose from their own members a president, secretary, and treasurer. The first mention of a mayor for the borough occurred in 1896; the mayor served, without payment, a term of office of two years. Other elected officers of the borough included at least one justice of the peace, a collector, and the commissioner of appeals in cases of taxation. The first meeting of the commission was held on April 15, 1882, at which time Walther Luttgen was elected as president, F.H. Hahn as secretary, and William H. Hood as treasurer.

The nonelected officials of the borough were then appointed by the mayor with the consent of a majority vote of the council, as long as a quorum was present. This was also necessary for the passing of legislation. However, the presence of all the commissioners was necessary to pass an ordinance. The appointed offices included a borough attorney, physician, engineer, recorder, overseer of the poor, superintendent of highways, and marshals for the borough, as needed. The borough of Linden did not have an overseer of the poor until 1897, when Smith

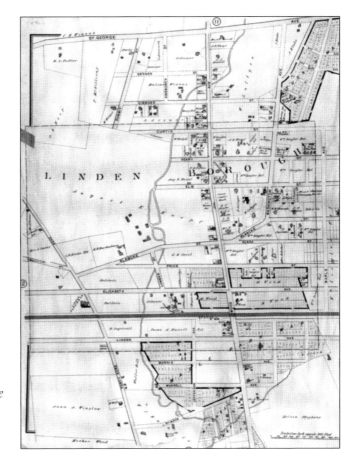

MAP OF BOROUGH OF LINDEN 1899–C. 1900. The Borough of Linden was incorporated in 1882 from the center of the township. It encompassed the downtown area from Curtis Street to the train station. The thick grey line depicts the railroad tracks. (Courtesy Morton Weitzman.)

F. Roll received the office. He resigned in 1898, only to be reappointed that same year. He served until 1900.

The board of health was organized on January 7, 1899, and at that time, its members were the seven incumbents of the offices of mayor and councilmen. The term of office was four years, but the terms were staggered so that new members were appointed each year. The board of health was extremely active, mainly because of the large number of complaints presented to it. The closeness of properties in the borough tended to create more controversies than might occur in a farming community.

In 1916, an infantile paralysis epidemic gripped Linden, and the board of health instituted precautions to prevent its spread. The *History of Linden* manuscript also states:

> The Township would furnish a day officer and the borough a night officer to be stationed at the railroad station not to allow non-resident children under sixteen years of age to stop at Linden, and any attempting to do so were to be turned back.

The board of health also engaged a nurse during the epidemic. In 1918, the Spanish flu epidemic prompted the New Jersey Board of Health to close schools, churches, theaters, and all places where people might congregate.

LINDEN POLICE CAR, 1925. This photograph shows an example of one of the early automobiles used by the Linden Police Department. (Courtesy Frank Deubel.)

At the first meeting of the borough commission on April 15, 1882, Constable Milton Clay Lowden was appointed to enforce the borough ordinances. He was later appointed marshal (chief of police), a position from which he resigned on September 30, 1896. On January 21, 1907, John L. Titus succeeded Lowden, followed by John Hughes as the next marshal. Sebastian Petrus was appointed to the job in May 1907. Soon, Petrus began serving as the day marshal and Charles W. Miles as the night marshal. In 1921, Miles was promoted, and Charles Bettle was added to the force of three men. On March 1, 1921, a council ordinance authorized a police department with further additions to the force. The last marshal to be appointed was Fred Wagner. The entire borough police force consolidated with the township police to form the City of Linden police force in 1925.

The borough's fire department was formed June 27, 1905, with a Mr. Huston appointed as chief and a Mr. Donaldson as assistant chief. The personnel of the department consisted solely of volunteers. Also in 1905, the borough asked the Linden Tanning Company, located on Stiles Street at Elizabeth Avenue and the railroad tracks, if it would blow its whistle for five long blasts in case of a fire within the borough. By 1914, the fire department's members numbered 32 men.

Gas lamps were in use on the streets of the borough as early as 1892, and Joe Kalligan was employed to tend the 12 lamps on Wood Avenue. In 1897, the borough established a five-year contract with the Elizabethtown Gas Company for 21 gas lamps. In 1902, this number grew to 43 gas lamps. In 1913, the borough contracted for 40 electric lamps with the electric company. Another 40 gas lamps were kept in service until they were replaced with electric lamps upon the consolidation of the borough and township.

On November 26, 1901, borough officials met with township officials to discuss the advisability of constructing a joint sewer, but it was not until July 31, 1905, that civil engineer J.L. Bauer was asked to furnish plans showing the cost of the proposed sewer. On April 17, 1909, a special election was held to raise funds for the project. Of the 50 votes cast, 49 were in favor of issuing $28,000 in bonds to cover the percentage agreed to by the borough.

Shortly after the incorporation of the borough, a building boom occurred, and prospective buyers came in from New York City by the trainfull. The borough of Linden became the residence of many well-to-do New Yorkers who commuted by train to their places of business. With the development of the area, the value of the borough of Linden as a residential district rose dramatically.

The first meeting of the borough commission was held in the "Academy of Arts and Sciences" on the property of Walther Luttgen. When Luttgen declined the position of borough commissioner in 1884, the commission then met at Fred Blancke's house until the year 1890. They also met at Edward Gulager's home, and in 1895, the commission rented the real estate office of H.W. Gesner as a meeting place. Following that, they met at the Titus E. and Zucher Hotel until the year 1908, at the office of W.H. Donaldson on Wood Avenue near Elizabeth Avenue, and in 1913, at Henry B. Hardenburg's home.

H.B. Hardenburg came to Linden in the late 1800s and established himself in a roomy house where School No. 8 now stands. He lived there until 1912, when he purchased the Cole home on Wood Avenue between Elm and Henry Streets. That house has since been destroyed by fire and another building erected in its place. Hardenburg served on the borough council in 1898, and in 1899, he was elected mayor, a position he held until 1920. He was also active in the social life of the community and served as president of the Linden Country Club for a number of years. In the business community, Hardenburg brought the H. Hardenburg Novelty Manufacturing Company, a firm he was connected with in Brooklyn for nearly 50 years, to Linden during the 1920s. He later sold his share of the business, which was located on West Elizabeth Avenue, and retired. The Wesley and Winter Stationery Company was then located at that site through the late 1940s. In 1944, Hardenburg's son H.B. Hardenburg Jr. had his residence at 23 West Elm Street.

On March 31, 1914, property that included a building and a barn in the rear, was purchased from Oscar Gesner for the purpose of constructing a borough hall at the corner of Wood and Blancke Streets. The present City Hall now occupies the site. The barn was converted into a firehouse by Frank Manuzza at a cost of $1,125 and was first occupied on July 15, 1916. Prior to this date, a building that was located on Elizabeth Avenue and rented for $5 per month was used as the firehouse. The borough did not erect any further public buildings.

The borough also purchased lot numbers 5, 6, 7, and 8 in Block 9 on the assessment map from Julia M. Gesner for $11. The land was to be used as a playground, located on the eastern side of Curtis Street between Wood Avenue and Ainsworth Street.

Some of the early residents living around the Pennsylvania Railroad station included members of the Wood, Winans, Roll, and Stimson families, but a number of other residents came to Linden from New York City via the railroad, including the Blancke, Luttgen, Knopf, Miner, Cole, and Ziegler families. These families were chiefly responsible for the development of the community around the railroad depot; in fact, close to three-quarters of the area was owned by just three men: Walther Luttgen, Ferdinand Blancke, and Meeker Wood.

Walther Luttgen, for whom Luttgen Place is named, made his fortune in financial operations on Wall Street in New York City. He purchased several large tracts of land, which were maintained as his estate, in Linden. In addition to building his home, Luttgen provided recreational facilities to his community in the form of a building once the home of the Linden Country Club and now used as the Moose Lodge. Luttgen donated land for the Grace Church and, from time to time, worked on his own pet projects, such as a kindergarten and private school. It is interesting to note that it was Luttgen who provided a macadamized road to his dock at Tremley Point, where he kept a yacht that he used to commute to New York City. After leaving Linden, Luttgen retired to a country estate in Connecticut.

Ferdinand Blancke was born in Minden, Germany on January 31, 1831 to Fredrick Blancke and Anna Snider; he died in Linden on June 16, 1901 at the age

LINDEN COUNTRY CLUB. Owned by Walther Luttgen, his private school, the Academy, had its classes here. The Linden Library was housed here due to help from the Rotary. In later years, it became home to the Loyal Order of Moose, Linden Lodge, No. 913. (Postcard courtesy L. Yeats.)

of 70. Blancke came to New York City from Germany in 1854 and established a lunchroom at 97 Cedar Street. He was married to the former Caroline Brah, who died in 1895, and the couple had four children: Ferdinand Jr., Herman, Emma, and Henry Louis. Blancke purchased large tracts of land in Linden when it was still a farming area and resold them later, thereby accumulating considerable resources. Blancke then purchased the Flaacke estate in the western section, north of Stiles Street. The Flaacke farm was noted for the great variety, quality, and quantity of fine fruits growing there and especially for its large apple, plum, and blackberry orchards. The produce grown on the farm was often among the prizewinners at state and county fairs. Grapes were also raised, not only in the vineyards, but in a specially constructed conservatory, as well. These were sold to Delmonico's in New York City for $1 per pound. Other fruits and many garden vegetables, as well as hay, grain, and feed were also shipped to the New York markets from Linden. After Blancke acquired the Flaacke property in Linden, he raised fresh vegetables there for his own restaurants in New York City.

Politics also claimed some of Blancke's attention. He was elected to the General Assembly from Union County in 1870 and 1871 and again in 1875. This was a time when intensive truck farming was the means of support for most of his Linden constituents. Blancke later sold the majority of his own holdings in the borough to August I. Knopf.

LINDEN NATIONAL BANK, 1902. This is a very scarce bank note. Only 47,000 large-size notes were printed with this bank title. According to the Hickman-Oakes National Banknotes Catalog, this is "an R-4 bank with only $8,950 size outstanding as of July 1935." The signatures are purple and rubberstamped. (Courtesy Alex Dimitrovski.)

Blancke's son Henry Louis was born in Brooklyn in 1862. He and his wife Harriet Louise had four sons—Harry F., who moved to Havana, Cuba; Edward Raymond; C. Dudley; and Wilbur—and two daughters—Mrs. A.H. Dabb, who resided at 26 West Curtis Street; and Mrs. A.M. Stevens of Miami, Florida. Henry L. Blancke has always been foremost among those who took an active part in local affairs. A tablet in School No. 1 testifies that Blancke was the vice president of the school board at the time of its erection. He served on the school board for many years and was later appointed custodian of school funds. He was one of the organizers of the Linden National Bank (which became known as the Linden National Bank and Trust Company) and the Linden Improvement Company, and he was secretary of the Fidelity Building and Loan, until poor health forced his retirement. Henry L. Blancke was also connected with the firm of Henry B. Hehrman and Son of New York City for 35 years. He was active in the social life of the community as well; he was one of the organizers of the Linden Country Club, where he served as a trustee for many years, and he was a member of Linden Lodge No. 2, Knights of Pythias.

Meeker Wood, the father of Fred M. Wood, was one of the residents of the "highway" now known as Wood Avenue. He served Linden as its postmaster and supplied fuel for the locomotives, which pulled trains over the single-track railroad that ran through the center of town. In those days, wood was the favorite fuel for locomotives, and the engines that puffed their way in and out of Linden were topped with large smokestacks.

The Linden National Bank, built in 1919, opened its doors at the corner of Wood Avenue at Elizabeth Avenue on February 4, 1920. It was a "Bank of Progress" as the first bank in Linden, and its officers were Frank G. Newell, president; H.B. Hardenburg, vice president; George L. Molson, vice president;

Forrest H. Farmer, cashier; Jean E. Muller, assistant cashier; and Stephen A. Gassler, assistant cashier. The bank's board of directors included F.R. Anderson, H.D. Banta, Harold DePew, F.H. Farmer, H.B. Hardenburg, George L. Molson, and F.G. Newell. The branch office at 201 North Wood Avenue opened in 1926, the 1158 East St. Georges Avenue office opened in 1935, and an office at St. Georges Avenue and DeWitt Terrace opened in 1949.

Linden's growth during the years following the formation of the city was steady. Between 1926 and 1929 Linden industries were expanded and enlarged. Then the stock market crash in Autumn 1929 brought seven long years of depression. April 1951 witnessed the closing of both the National Bank and Trust Co. and the State Bank. The former reopened after one week as the Linden National Bank with new management. In December of the same year, it was taken over by the Trust Co.

The depositors at the Linden National Bank did not lose on their accounts and at the State Bank, dividends of 50 percent were paid out. From 1951 to 1954 the Trust Co. was the only banking institution remaining in Linden. In 1955, Community Bank came to North Wood Avenue with Arthur R. Croucher, Manuel Margolies, and Ben Rosen. The bank was very successful, with a second branch at the corner of Stiles Street and St. Georges Avenue. In 1969 Community merged with the State Bank of Rahway and became known as Community State Bank and Trust Company.

Stonewall Savings and Loan Association was established in April 1921. Leon A. Watson was one of its founders and served as president and chairman of the board of directors until April 1960. The board of directors in 1961 consisted of the following members who had served continuously from the year indicated after their name: Joseph S. Lindabury, counselor at law, since 1926; H.H. Zeitlin, medical doctor, since 1930; Louis Weitzman, assistant tax collector, since 1931; Emanuel Margulies, president, Community Bank, since 1932; John P. Voynick, retired, since 1936; A.F. Krutzner Jr., executive vice president of Stonewall, since 1944; Elvin D. Palermo, real estate and insurance, since 1947; Caroline B. Guinan, retired, since 1947; Morris Levine, real estate and insurance, since 1948; A. Edward Mrozek, auto dealer, since 1951; John J. Horan, lumber dealer, since 1961; and Dominick Caruso, retailer, since 1961. Columbia Bank bought Stonewall in 1981 and is thriving today.

The early part of this century saw marathons of all varieties born in the minds of young people and Linden was no exception. Joseph Loitsch, along with James Maye, Joseph Tomarchik, and Chris Wendell, had one goal—to bicycle across the country. On June 28, 1913, the boys started their trip to California on 75-pound bikes costing them each $115, an exorbitant price, to say the least, in 1913! The event was the talk of Linden when the boys departed; soon, however, spirits fell as one after another dropped from the quest. Loitsch made it as far as Ohio, some 510 miles, when he felt he had had enough and returned. Only one of the boys, James Maye, made the entire trip and became the first man to cross the country on a bicycle. In each town he passed through, Maye obtained the signatures of the

STATE BANK. This bank was located on St. Georges Avenue. (Courtesy UCHS.)

mayors. He also pedaled to the capital of each state and collected the governor's signature or seal. He even met President Woodrow Wilson.

After interviewing Loitsch for a Kean College research paper, Morris Leone wrote the following item:

> Loitsch and Maye lost contact with each other and in fact had assumed the other had passed away. It was not until Linden joined the rest of the nation in celebrating the Bicentennial that many questions were answered. The Linden Leader ran a series of articles on memorable events in the history of the City and in one of the articles traced the story of James Maye and revealed his 1976 residence as neighboring Rahway, New Jersey. Loitsch still resided in Linden. At that time he was 81 years old. A short time later, the two old friends, Loitsch and Maye were reunited to reminisce "old times" and renew an old and lasting friendship.

Loitsch and his sister Mamie also shared their memories of Linden with Morris Leone, recalling how their family lived in a "small shack on Hussa Street. At the time there were woods down to Maple Avenue."

Loitsch also remembered "taking up the sidewalks because of the hobos." Believe it or not, there was a time when residents of Linden had to pull their sidewalks in at night to save them from being stolen. During these days, the Pennsylvania Railroad was on a level with Wood Avenue. Before the advent of concrete sidewalks, Linden residents used to build wooden walks in front of their homes, but for a long time, many mysteriously disappeared at night. A check by the town constable showed that hobos, who had set themselves up in Linden's freight yards, took the planks for use as firewood. Residents then began building their wooden walks in small sections so that at night, the pieces could be picked up and taken indoors. Borough officials subsequently found a good way of ridding the town of its hobo nuisance by passing an ordinance that provided for "a jail sentence on the county prison farm for all vagrants henceforth found in Linden." Hobos gave Linden a wide berth after that.

After the development of the first successful steam locomotive in the United States by John Stevens (of Stevens Institute of Technology fame), the New Jersey Railroad began laying track for a main line between New York and Philadelphia in 1831. Railroads were built in small segments. Each segment was chartered as an individual railroad and then joined to the parent. By 1835, the first railway line went through the Linden area of Elizabethtown. Trains between New York and Philadelphia soon began stopping at Linden's railroad station, which was named Wheatsheaf but called "Wood Station" by locals. It was Ferdinand Blancke who finally had the name of the station officially changed to Linden. As early as 1851, there were two tracks from Rahway to New York and one track from Rahway to Trenton. By 1896, there were four tracks passing through Linden.

On August 18, 1903, an injunction was obtained to restrict the Pennsylvania Railroad Company, which had acquired the New Jersey Railroad, from laying more than four tracks until the Dark Lane (Park Avenue) ground-level crossing was eliminated. Eight years later, on January 5, 1911, the township committee received a communication from the Pennsylvania Railroad Company regarding the construction of additional tracks and an overhead crossing on Dark Lane; both soon became realities. The roadway is now called the Park Avenue Bridge.

Due to the lowering of the grade of Wood Avenue and the surrounding area to be under the railroad tracks, the station was razed. The unusual orientation of the station (with its end facing the tracks) allowed a trunk line for mail delivery to run along Wood Avenue. The current railroad station on Wood Avenue was built in 1911 in a Spanish revival style. Stucco and brick were usually only employed in domestic architecture, which makes this building unique among the railroad stations of Union County. After the Pennsylvania Railroad (PRR) merged with the New York Central in 1968, the company's name was changed to Penn Central. On April 1, 1976, the state took over the bankrupt railroad and maintained control until 1983, when New Jersey Transit acquired the commuter rail operations.

The Elizabethtown & Somerville Railroad, predecessor to the Central New Jersey (CNJ) Railroad, began service in Elizabethtown with horse-powered trains on August 13, 1839. On January 1, 1842, the first locomotive on the CNJ, *The Eagle*, ran from Elizabethport to Plainfield. In 1847, this line became the Central New Jersey Railroad, and by 1854, it was linked to the Baltimore & Ohio Railroad. In 1871, the Elizabethport & Perth Amboy Line, a branch of the Central Railroad, passed through Linden.

It connected with the New York & Long Branch Railroad, and while of some importance to passenger trade, its main value to Linden was serving industries along the waterfront. The Tremley Station on the Central Railroad line was built on the site of the old Tremley homestead. The station was also used as a post office for the area.

The Baltimore & Ohio Railroad, also created in 1839, was a line used solely for the transportation of freight. The tracks crossed the northeasterly section of Linden, connected to Staten Island by a bridge over the Arthur Kill, and ran into the main line of the Central Railroad. In 1905, the Linden township committee passed an ordinance that permitted the Baltimore & Ohio to construct permanent bridges over both Linden Avenue and Elizabeth Avenue, both of which still exist today.

PENNSYLVANIA RAILROAD STATION. The station was built in 1910 on the site where it is still presently located. (Courtesy L. Yeats.)

In 1894, an ordinance permitting a trolley car line along St. Georges Avenue was passed, but the franchise was never exercised. In 1913, the Linden Trolley was also granted a franchise, which also never went into effect. However, starting in March 1905, the "Fast Line" trolley franchise ran from Newark to Perth Amboy. Lou Fogel, who had the pleasure of riding the trolley a few times, wrote about it in a manuscript of his remembrances of Linden: "It was really fast. We would board it at Wood Avenue and Tremley Point."

And then there was the "Short Line." As early as 1903, Trenton & New Brunswick Railroad saw a need for a route between Trenton and Newark. On April 2, 1904, Public Service took up the idea and sponsored the New Jersey Short Line Railroad. The Short Line did quite a bit of work before it finally went broke in 1908, grading most of the road and furnishing it with bridges between Bayway (Elizabeth) and Bonhamtown.

Public Service decided to revive the scheme by purchasing the Short Line and the Trenton & New Brunswick Railroad. Construction resumed on August 12, 1912, under the title of Trenton Terminal Railroad. Some difficulty was experienced below Bayway when it was discovered that the land was composed of a soft, spongy mass upon which it was difficult to lay track. A heavy layer of cinder ballast rectified the situation. Over the Rahway River, engineers erected a "jack-knife"–type drawbridge.

Another mode of transportation soon became possible in the area with the arrival in Linden of Frank S. Villani and Felice Beviano.

Born in Italy, Frank S. Villani came to Linden from Dupont, Pennsylvania. He enlisted in the army during World War I and served in France. Upon his return, he was employed by Merck and was a volunteer fireman in Newark. In 1919, Villani purchased a small jitney (a rebuilt truck), which he called the "5 cent Jitney Express."

He founded the Villani Bus Company, and soon his vehicles serviced the route between Linden and Elizabeth. Early in the 1920s, Villani also began the first school bus service in Linden. He and his wife Palma ran the bus company, and also opened an Italian grocery at 115 South Wood Avenue, all while raising three sons and five daughters.

The grocery store closed during World War II, when importing came to a halt. But Villani expanded his regular bus service from local to long-distance and charter runs in 1936, and he continued to run the company for more than 60 years. He was also active in community organizations. Villani was a charter member of the Elks Lodge #1960 and a member of the Loyal Order of Moose Lodge #913, the John Russell Wheeler Veterans of Foreign Wars Post #1397, the American Legion Post #102, and the American Italian Club (all of Linden), as well as a member of the Sociate di Buonalbergo of Newark and the New Jersey Motor Bus Association.

In 1960, Palma passed away, but the family pulled together to keep things running smoothly. The 1960s brought more change to the family when Frank remarried and had another son. His eldest son Diodato became president of the bus company, while brother Carmine was named secretary and put in charge of the shop. When founder Frank Villani died at age 92, he was survived by sons Diodato, Carmine, Frank, and Francesco, and daughters Clara (Troiano), Rosalie (Bosco), Joanna (Colucci), Carmella (Sadry), and Aida (St. John). The family boasted 15 grandchildren and 9 great-grandchildren.

In 1914, Felice and Giroloma Beviano left Dupont, Pennsylvania with their seven children—Onofrio, Joseph, Raymond, Frank, Anthony, Mary, Mamie, and Grace—and moved to a 19-room house on top of the hill on Wood Avenue, between St. Georges Avenue and Gesner Street.

This homestead was the original location of Beviano Chartered Service, and the first six-passenger open-window vehicle in the city was parked in the Bevianos' backyard. Felice was issued a permit to run this bus in town and to Elizabeth (the #44 Edgar Road route), but eventually, service was expanded with the influx of new residents. In 1923, the family-run operation was moved to 1103 North Wood Avenue. Beviano stated, "There were more than 6 different bus companies competing on this #44 Edgar Road now and the rivalry was fierce." Beviano got to keep running this route until 1984.

When World War II began, the Beviano Chartered Service supported the war effort by transporting troops to the Bayonne and Jersey City seaports and other locations. In the following years, the company expanded to charter service and school transportation, and Beviano's fleet size rose to an average of 25 to 30 buses. In addition to the successful #44 Edgar Road route, Felice added the #10 Cranford Kenilworth route to his company's services.

When 1953 came around, the labor unions entered Linden. Felice Beviano, however, refused to give in to them because he believed they "wanted to take his life-long dreams and just crush them." He and his five sons held the unions off for eight months, standing guard at the front doors of the garage they had built. The family fought and won its battle. In 1955, Felice Beviano died; his son Giroloma was then in charge.

On a dark morning in 1968, an old bus parked in the rear of the garage caught fire from an electrical short in the wiring harness. This fire spread to the other buses that were parked nearby. Once the fire had spread, there was no chance of containing the flames that shot through the roof up to 40 feet in the air. Linden's finest did all they could to contain the situation, but all the buses in the fleet were lost to the fire.

Anthony Beviano, who was running the office at the time, called on all the bus companies in the area to help out with spare buses so that customers would not be affected by the fire. And at 4:45 a.m., ten buses were lined up outside the charred building waiting for drivers to begin their routes.

In the fall of 1973, the five sons of Felice and Giroloma Beviano retired and turned the operations over to their three sons, Philip, Joseph, and Raymond. In the spring of 1975, the new owners had saved enough money to purchase a new bus from General Motors Bus Division. Also assisting in the business's operations were three great-grandsons, Philip, Joseph, and Todd. In 1976, the company embarked on a new line service that ended at the Meadowlands Sports Complex and Racetrack, with pickup points in Rahway, Linden, and Elizabeth. Due to a family decision, the company came to a close in 1984. The family decided to break up the business; according to Beviano, there were no other reasons for the closing.

PETERS-ELIZABETHTOWN-LINDEN BUS LINE, 1922. This was one of 12 bus lines in the area. Villani Bus Lines and Beviano Bus Lines were located in Linden. (Courtesy UCHS.)

7. THE CITY OF LINDEN: UNITED WE STAND

Incorporated on January 1, 1925, the city of Linden conformed to the mayor-council form of government, and George McGillvray was chosen as the city's first mayor. At the organization meeting of the common council, Leon A. Watson was elected by his colleagues as council president, and the councilmen, each representing a ward, drew lots to determine the length of their respective terms. Thomas A. Archipley, John J. Vanderwall Sr., Edward M. Wallace, and James T. Bersey drew three-year terms, while William Nickola, Charlie Kasper, Stephen Pekar, and Harry McDaniel drew two-year terms. The terms of the councilmen were staggered so that there would always be experienced councilmen serving with the newly elected councilmen. Since the legal voters of Linden failed to elect a city clerk, Thomas H. Sullivan was appointed to that position. The mayor, with the approval of the council, appointed Joseph Ross as city treasurer for three years, and D. Banta was appointed to the office of collector for one year. The assessor's office was expanded from a one-man office to a board consisting of three men: Albert Weber, Albert H. Dabb, and Philip Litwinoff. Appointed with the new government were the members of the Board of Education, who had been elected prior to the formation of the city in accordance with state laws in 1925. Fred McGillvray was appointed overseer of roads and garbage removal at a salary of $6 per day, and William H. Moore received the appointment of overseer of the poor on May 20, 1925, to fill the vacancy caused by the death of William T. Day. The board of health consisted of the following appointed members: John Lambert (one-year term), Dr. H. Page Hough (two-year term), Henry A. Pennoyer (three-year term), Charles Nichols (four-year term), and Abraham Weinberg (four-year term). In April 1925, two additional men were appointed to this board: Dr. A.H. Barr (two-year term) and A. Kaufman (three-year term).

With the new city government, old political divisions were soon forgotten. Three public buildings (excluding schools) were constructed in a period of about a year. The first was a city hall, which was formally dedicated on September 30, 1930 and brought to Linden the honor of housing the 5th District Court. The bill forming this district (comprising Linden, Rahway, Clark, Roselle, Cranford, and Garwood) was passed by the state on April 16, 1931, and Lewis C. Lehman Jr. of Roselle was appointed as judge. Land was also purchased for the construction of a municipal garage building, which is still located on the corner of Wood Avenue and Munsell Avenue.

In 1925, the city council of the City of Linden adopted an ordinance establishing a paid fire department to take the place of the volunteer firemen of both the borough and the township. The City of Linden currently has four firehouses. Firehouse No. 1 was built in 1916 at Wood and Morris Avenues when the area was still Linden Township; it was remodeled in 1960. Firehouse No. 2 was built in 1946 at St. Georges Avenue and DeWitt Terrace, No. 3 was built in 1929 at Elizabeth and Chandler Avenues, and No. 4 was constructed in the Tremley section on South Wood Avenue in 1979.

George McGillvray served as the first mayor of the City of Linden from 1925 to 1926, and he was followed by Albert Weber, who served the 1927–1928 term. McGillvray was re-elected to serve in 1929–1930. In November 1931, Jules Verner was named acting mayor upon the death of James B. Furber, the 62-year-old mayor elect, who died one week after the election was held.

Furber had an interesting career. He was born in Allegany, Michigan, and attended Mt. Olivet and Grand Rapids business colleges. He worked as a traveling salesman and district manager for the National Cash Register Company, until at age 42 he began a law career with the New Jersey Bar. In 1917, Furber was the general manager of Regina Corporation. He held the office of mayor twice in

GEORGE MCGILLVRAY. He was the first mayor of the City of Linden in 1925. He was also elected for the years 1926, 1929, and 1930. (Courtesy L. Yeats.)

POSING POLITICIANS. From left to right are New Jersey State Senator Bill Bradley, New York Senator Patrick Mohnahan, Linden Council President Edward Murowski, and Mayor John T. Gregorio (Courtesy Pat Malicher.)

Rahway, as a Republican from 1905 to 1907 and as an Independent from 1922 to 1924. In Rahway in 1917, a special election took place to adopt commission rule and disband the council form that had been in effect since incorporation. Under this new system of government, three commissioners would govern the city rather than a mayor and councilmen. Another commissioner at that time was David Trembley.

Arriving in Linden in 1924, James Furber handled the affairs of the Berlant Development Company as the company's president and also established law offices in the Linden National Bank Building. Furber had won the mayoral election by 95 votes, beating out the incumbent mayor George McGillvray. Interestingly, Furber and McGillvray shared a grandchild. Furber's daughter Helen Josephine married Mc Gillvray's son Fred, and the couple's daughter Marion (Smith) was born in 1902. In addition to winning the office of mayor, Furber was also elected vice president of the Linden Lions a week before he died. After Furber's death, his remains were removed to the Linden City Hall to lie in state and were in the charge of the City of Linden until interment. The city also provided a police detail to act as guard of honor.

The following mayors have governed the city of Linden since that time: Myles J. McManus (1933–1943), H. Roy Wheeler (1944–1952), William Hurst

(1953–1964), Alexander Wrigley (1965–1966), John T. Gregorio (1967–1983), George Hudak (1983–1986), Paul Werkmeister (1987–1990), and John T. Gregorio (1991–present).

The current mayor of Linden John T. Gregorio's first elected position was that of first ward councilman in Linden in 1964. He was also a member of the New Jersey State Assembly for four years and the New Jersey State Senate for six years. Additionally, Gregorio served as a member of the Juvenile Conference Committee, the Linden Volunteer Ambulance Squad, and the Union County Psychiatric Committee. He was the director of the Metropolitan Regional Council and the New Jersey State League of Municipalities and a member of the United States Conference of Mayors, the Union County Conference of Mayors, and the New Jersey Narcotic Officers Association. He was also named chairman of the Metropolitan Regional Council Water Pollution Agency and has participated in a number of local organizations, including the Knights of Columbus, the Kiwanis Club, and the American Legion.

A Navy veteran of World War II, John T. Gregorio established the House of Flowers florist shop in Linden in 1950. He and his wife, the former Marie Pernicone, have a daughter, Jodi Pucillo, who is the manager of House of Flowers; a son, John Jr., who is the president of JTG and Sons Scaffolding, Inc; and seven grandchildren: Maria Colicchio, Dante Pucillo, Jianna Marie, Jenna Rose, Jordanna Alexa, Jannia Alyssandra, and John T. Gregorio III.

MAYOR H. ROY WHEELER. He was an LHS graduate of 1923, and attended Newark College for Engineering. He held construction engineer and surveyor's licenses. He completed Myles McManus's unexpired term. He was known for his poise, tact, low voice, sincere smile, and great memory for names.(Drake)

During the difficult years of the Great Depression, the mayor and council of Linden officially acknowledged the seriousness of the demand for relief workers by forming a committee to deal with the problem on December 4, 1930. This action mobilized all relief workers into one group to assist the overseer of the poor. The relief committee included members of churches and civic clubs, city officials, and private citizens and was incorporated as the Linden Welfare Federation (also known as the Home Service Organization). An unofficial study conducted by the *Linden Observer* in 1931 estimated that 1,300 people, or two-thirds of the city, were unemployed.

Further assistance to the overseer of the poor came with the January 1931 inauguration of the Municipal Emergency Bureau, which maintained a file containing the names of all unemployed people along with their work experience. In addition, Mayor Jules Verner called for a meeting of the heads of local industries to encourage them to aid in the local unemployment situation by offering work to Linden's citizens. A traveling soup kitchen, inaugurated by the Lions Club and then taken over by the city, was another measure of relief.

Bonus Army marchers, who traveled through Linden on their way to demonstrate in Washington, D.C. in 1931, were fed at the soup kitchen before continuing on their journey. In the spring of 1932, more than 20,000 veterans of World War I, unemployed and in desperate financial straits due to the Depression, arrived in Washington, D.C. as Bonus Marchers. They demanded passage of a bill introduced by Representative Wright Patman providing for immediate payment of their World War I bonus. The Senate defeated the Patman bill on June 17, 1932. The marchers refused to leave. On July 28, President Herbert Hoover ordered Douglas MacArthur to evict them forcibly. MacArthur had army troops set their camps on fire to drive the veterans from the city. Hoover was much criticized by the public for the severity of his response. The nation sacrificed many nonessential commodities during the Great Depression, but the products coming out of Linden, most significantly chemicals and oil, were considered some of the country's basic needs.

In an attempt to satisfy the health needs of local citizens, the Linden Community Hospital Association was incorporated in 1928 and purchased an entire block in the heart of the residential district—"Block 72 of the Sunnyside Gardens development which was right on the golf links and facing the High School on St. Georges Avenue"—so that the city could build a community hospital. The Linden Community Hospital never came to pass, and Linden residents continued to be served by the hospitals in the surrounding area.

The Linden Volunteer Ambulance Organization was organized in 1945 by 11 people and began operations with a converted hearse-ambulance and a headquarters on Price Street. This dedicated group was awarded an Americanism Citation for Meritorious Service by the B'nai B'rith in 1959, and is now located at its new home on Stiles Street next to the railroad overpass. In the year 2002 the site is undergoing renovations to update the facility.

KAY SAFFER AND PERRY LEIB. The two pose with the marchers re-enacting Washington's march through New Jersey. Jack in the Box of Roselle is visible behind the group. To the left would have been the site of the Wheatsheaf Tavern 200 years prior. (Courtesy Esther Leib.)

A shining star in Linden, the Center for Hope Hospice is located at 176 Hussa Street in a facility that once housed St. Elizabeth's Convent. Founded in the late 1970s by Peggy Coloney, R.N., and Father Charles Hudson, the center abides by its mission to provide physical, emotional, and spiritual support to all individuals facing the challenges of a life-limiting illness, without regard to their ability to pay.

Father Hudson was honored for his service to mankind and his love for all people with the esteemed Martin Luther King Award on January 20, 1997, just one day before his death. In his acceptance speech, Hudson told a story of a young boy who played a game with a small piece of a broken mirror. The boy would catch the light and reflect it into dark places. Father Hudson referred to himself as a fragment of a mirror whose whole design and shape were unknown. He stated, "I am not the light but I try to reflect the light into the dark places of this world and change some things in some people. Perhaps then, others may see and do likewise."

The original Linden Library, which was sponsored by the Linden Rotary Club, was located in the stable wing of the Linden Country Club (now Moose Hall), opened in March 1928, and eventually resulted in the establishment of the public library. The first library board was composed of H.B. Ashwell, president; William

Palermo, treasurer; E.J. Perot, secretary; trustees Dr. H.M. Glasston and Thomas H. Sullivan; and ex-officio members Mayor Albert F. Weber and D.A. Howell, supervising principal of Linden schools. Miss Viola R. Maihl was the librarian for many years and was known for her organization and love of history. The Reverend Ellistoin J. Perot, rector of Grace Episcopal Church, was the most active proponent of the library movement and was key in moving the main branch to a storefront at 428 North Wood Avenue in the 1930s. At that time, there were three branch libraries: the Chandler Avenue branch; the Grier Avenue branch, located at 2402 East Edgar Road; and the Main Street branch, located at 3102 Tremley Point Road. In 1955, the library adopted a long-range plan that called for the erection of two new branch library buildings and a change of emphasis at the main library to a strong information and research center. The openings of the Sunnyside and Dill Avenue branches were part of that plan. In 1960, there were a few separate branches of the Linden Library: the main library, still located at 31 East Henry Street; the Sunnyside branch at Edgewood Road; the Chandler Avenue branch at 1009 Chandler Avenue; and the Dill Avenue branch, which replaced the Chandler Avenue branch. In January 2001, plans for both the Dill Avenue and Sunnyside branch libraries changed. The Dill Avenue building, in time, will be razed and the site redeveloped to provide senior citizen housing. The Sunnyside branch is currently undergoing renovations to become offices for the

FIRE CHIEF FRANK MILLER. He stands in the lobby of the Plaza Theater with a display for fire safety. (Courtesy LFD, Lukenda.)

Linden Board of Education. Both will still offer public reading rooms at the new sites.

The president of Linden's first library board, H.B. Ashwell, also founded the *Linden Observer* newspaper in May 1920. Less than a year later, Ashwell, who had been publishing the paper as a sideline, turned it over to the Kempson brothers of Roselle Park, and Eber Hall Kempson became the publisher in 1922. In 1933, Eber Kempson left Linden, but his wife continued to produce the *Observer* for nearly a year. In 1935, she sold the paper to young Morris Winetsky, who was said to be a brilliant writer. Winetsky changed the whole style of the paper, giving it a "big-time" flavor. He edited the *Observer* for seven years and then sold it to the Union Register Company. However, the Linden Observer Publishing Company bought the paper only six months later, in May 1940. Grant W. Bauer was the president of the Observer Company, which also owned the *Union Register* in Union, and Edmund J. McCormick, formerly of *Time* magazine, was the vice president. Peter M. Bosco, who began as a reporter with the *Observer*, soon became the sports editor and, in September 1939, was made editor of the paper. The newspaper's office was located at 6 East Blancke Street.

In June 1955, the one-year-old *Linden Record* was combined with the *Linden Observer*. The *Linden News*, another weekly, was started in 1927 by Daniel Shulhafer. Mr. Leslie L. Rood became the publisher and his daughter Elizabeth assumed the editorship. The newspaper's office was at 11 West Blancke Street. Herman Mopsick later became owner-editor of the weekly *Linden News-Observer*. Mopsick also served as principal of Linden High School in later years.

On September 19, 1962, the *Linden Leader* was founded by a group of independent Linden residents and business people. Herbert Jaffe and Murray Friedfeld were the original associate publishers. In September 1982, Walter Worrall of the Worrall Community Newspapers, Inc. purchased the paper from Asher Mintz of Suburban Publishing Corporation. Worrall Newspapers is a family-owned company that publishes 19 local weekly newspapers. In 1997, the name of the *Linden Leader* was changed to the *Spectator Leader*, and the publication now reports the local news of both Linden and Roselle.

A very popular and inexpensive form of entertainment in Linden during the first half of the twentieth century was the local movie houses. A *c.* 1929 advertisement for the Plaza Theatre in the *Linden Observer* stated, "Among the newer and better buildings in Linden is that which houses the Plaza Theatre—a popular show house presenting the latest lilts in the moving-and-talking picture world; seating 1300 persons, and fireproof." In conjunction with the excellent pictures shown there, the Plaza Theatre, opened in 1925, also showcased four acts of excellent vaudeville during the 1920s. The high-class entertainment was furnished for only a 5¢ increase on the price of a regular movie admittance. Three vaudeville performances were given each Sunday. Other Linden theatres included the Opera House, built in 1915 on the 100 block of Wood Avenue and later known as the Roxanne Theatre; and another at the corner of Chandler and St. Georges Avenues that showed movies until the mid-1940s.

In an interview with Morris Leone, Edward Huey, a science teacher at Soehl Junior High School during the 1970s, reminisced about his younger days in Linden, specifically about the fun of sneaking into the local movie house.

> Children would often go around the neighborhood looking for scraps of metal and when enough was collected they would go to Urbanowitz Brothers scrap metal yard and trade it in for a nickel. On Saturday one or two boys would have a nickel and go to the neighborhood movie house on Chandler Avenue. The building became the White Rock Baptist Church. After they went in, one of the boys would go to a side door and open it to let his friends in. The manager would try to catch them but in those days tickets were not sold . . . a person just paid the nickel and walked in. Therefore, the manager had no way of telling who paid and who did not.

THE LINDEN PLAZA THEATER, 1943. There was quite a crowd gathered for Hello Frisco. *(Courtesy L. Yeats, Andrea Amabile.)*

8. GOLDEN RULE DAYS

Linden's education history began in the days when it was still a part of Elizabethtown, and the first schooling was typically associated with individual religions and churches.

The Wheatsheaf School, which was in existence by 1750, was built at the junction of what is now St. Georges Avenue and Roselle Street, nearly opposite the Wheatsheaf Inn. Its first teacher was John Cotton. The schoolroom was said to be 7 feet high and heated by a heavy, wood-burning box stove in the center. In fact, the punishment administered to the unruly student required him or her to cut wood for the school's stove. The building was occupied until 1820, when a new schoolhouse was erected nearby, just north of the Wheatsheaf Inn. In 1853 Abram Ward, as schoolteacher, presided over a class of 55 students for a salary of $400 per year. In 1859, the trustees of the school charged $2 per year for tuition. In 1866 the Wheatsheaf School closed, but at the request of a Miss Tucker, the building was rented to her for six months as a private school.

Established in 1786, the Tremley Point School could be found on Morses Mill Road, and its first teachers included Russell Sargent, Robert Dennis, and Jesse Clark. In 1825, a new building was erected with the funds contributed by families in the neighborhood. The new school featured a platform for the teacher's desk and double desks for 16 children. The school's contributors also decided on its name—Union Seminary. Locally, however, the school was known as Hogtown School. Early school organization was in the hands of subscribers and only their children were in attendance. This system of control continued until 1842, when the state legislature established the Free Public School Act.

Two noteworthy private schools began in the late 1800s and were supported through the philanthropy of Linden resident Walther Luttgen, a native of Germany who came to the United States following the Civil War. Luttgen's estate stretched from St. Georges Avenue to Blancke Street and from Wood Avenue to Washington Avenue. A partner of banker August Belmont, Luttgen used a great portion of his own wealth to fund improvements in Linden. In the 1870s, he built the Academy of Arts and Sciences, housed in what is now the Moose Hall on Luttgen Place, and the Amelia Victoria Kindergarten, which he named for his wife.

The kindergarten, which held about 20 children, was established in a one-room bungalow several doors east of the present library, and it served the community for 40 years. Before the school opened, Luttgen had studied German kindergarten methods, and his institution was considered years ahead of its time. Although Luttgen was an Episcopalian, the school was nondenominational.

The Academy of Arts and Sciences, established for older children, lasted only a short time as a school but served as a center for community activities in the latter part of the nineteenth century. When Luttgen was elected president of the borough, part of this building, which was known as "the Casino," became a stable for the Luttgen estate, while another part of it became a home for the servants. The building was also known as the Linden Country Club, and in 1927, the Linden Library moved there.

In 1871, Linden's first public school building was constructed on Linden Avenue on land donated by Meeker Wood, and it took the place of the Shunpike and Stiles Street schools, which had been discontinued by the state when the New Jersey public school system was created. In 1875, the school was given the official title of Public School No. 1. By 1907, two years of high school classes had been added. On December 2, 1909, a tremendous fire burned the school down, and although firefighters were on the scene, the hoses they were using had been laid across a set of railroad tracks to the water source on the other side. An unexpected night train cut the hoses, and the building continued to burn. Until permanent facilities could be constructed, a temporary school was built at the corner of Munsell and Wood Avenues.

Between 1912 and 1924, there was a dramatic increase in the number of schoolchildren in the area, which led to the use of temporary and portable school buildings. These structures were erected on the site of the old Linden Avenue school during the summer of 1921. Part of one of these buildings may be the present-day McManus Hall on Wood Place.

In January 1903, the idea to build a new school for the Greater Elizabeth section was approved; most of the children in this community had been attending school in Elizabeth. The state board of education, however, did not approve the construction of the new school, so 39 pupils and a fifth teacher were added to School No. 1. In March 1904, plans were again considered for a school annex in Greater Elizabeth, and this time, the project was approved. All children under six years of age were to attend school in their districts. In 1905, Samuel Hedden purchased a house and opened it for school purposes. The school operated until election night in 1911, when the facility burned to the ground. Rooms were also rented on Edgar Road from a Judge Ober and a Mr. Frank, and these were in use until 1913, when the new School No. 3 was ready for occupancy.

The cornerstone of School No. 1 was laid on April 22, 1911. Located at 728 North Wood Avenue, the building was completed in 1912 at a cost of $100,000. The huge structure housed both elementary and high school students, and it was certified as a four-year high school by the state board of education. In 1957, the third-floor auditorium was closed. An addition was constructed in 1972.

SCHOOL NO.1. This postcard identifies the building as the new high school located at North Wood Avenue. (Courtesy L. Yeats.)

In February 1912, the school in Tremley was closed and plans were made to have its 30 children transported to the new School No. 1, which had opened earlier that winter. J.J. Savitz, the county superintendent, condemned the Tremley building in April of that year, and the children were transferred. Later in 1912, Tremley residents requested that a school be maintained in their district, and the old building was reopened, pending the erection of a new school.

Miss Lida M. Ebbert was appointed principal of School No. 1 in the spring of 1912. Plans for establishing a night school were discussed by the board about this time, but no decision was reached until the fall. On December 1, the first adult education program in Linden began, with a class of 27 students.

In 1912, the voters of the township decided to erect two new schools, one on South Wood Avenue (to be known as School No. 2) and one in Greater Elizabeth (School No. 3). Both would be six-room, brick buildings. The cornerstones of both schools were laid on Saturday, November 22, 1912, with all the appropriate ceremonies. In the spring of 1913, these schools opened and the school districts re-designated. School No. 2 was constructed at 1700 South Wood Avenue and Seventeenth Street, and additions were made to the original structure in 1919 and 1967 due to increased enrollment in the neighborhood.

School No. 3 was constructed at the corner of Grier Avenue and Dennis Place in 1912, and classes began in the spring of 1913. An addition was built in 1928. School No. 3 was the first school to have a Parent Teacher Association. The building still stands today but is not in use as a public school. It is now a private school known as the Christian Academy.

SCHOOL NO. 6. *The school was built in 1923 and is located at 619 Morris Avenue. (Courtesy L. Yeats.)*

The year 1914 brought a realization of the need for a school in the rapidly growing district around St. Georges and Chandler Avenues. A petition from the residents of this area revealed the fact that there were 250 children in this section and the need for a school building was, in fact, urgent. In the fall of 1914, voters were called together for a special election, and it was decided to build a school in this section at a cost not to exceed $50,000 for both the land and the building.

The cornerstone for what would become School No. 4 was laid in 1915, construction was begun shortly thereafter, and dedication services were held on January 8, 1916. Due to the increasing number of children in the neighborhood, an annex—it was to be a separate building on the Lampert Farm along Dill Avenue—was being planned as early as 1960. A new annex contains four grade classrooms and two kindergartens. Over time, enrollment numbers went down, so the original School No. 4 was converted into office space for the board of education in 1980. Apartments are now located at this site. The School No. 4 Annex was recently under construction to add more classrooms and a gymnasium; the building has taken on the new name of School No. 4 and reopened September 9, 2002.

At the time of World War I, Linden's growing student enrollment again required the construction of a new building. The cornerstone for Public School No. 5 was laid on September 18, 1920, and classes began in September 1921. An addition to the original building, located at 1014 Bower Street, was constructed in 1965.

School No. 6 was constructed in 1923 on the site of the first public school, which burned down in 1909. Faculty, students, and parents at School No. 6 officially welcomed a new symbol of their institution's and city's heritage when Principal Michael DeMicele dedicated a 4-by-24-foot mural, completed for the school, during the annual spring concert on May 12, 1988. The mural was commissioned by Virginia Sleiger, a second-grade teacher at School No. 6, as a recipient of the state-sponsored Teacher Recognition Award program. The three-panel work traces the growth and development not only of School No. 6 but also of Linden as a community. It was painted by famous sports illustrator Bil Canfield.

Because of the overcrowding at School No. 1, it was decided that a separate high school should be built, so land was purchased on St. Georges Avenue between Ainsworth and Summit Streets. The cornerstone was laid on October 10, 1924, and the school opened in 1925. Two additions to the high school were made, one in 1931 and the second in 1960. Two courses, the commercial and the general, were soon added to the original one-course program. Linden High School was one of the first high schools in New Jersey to become a member of the Middle States Association of Colleges and Secondary Schools, and it has been approved by that accrediting agency ever since. Lida M. Ebbert became the

MURAL AT SCHOOL NO. 9. Festivities surrounding the presentation of the mural in the lobby brought the attention of Linden to School No. 9. Principal James Waters welcomes superintendent of schools Americo Taranto, Governor Tom Kean, Mayor George Hudak, and Union County Superintendent of Schools Vito Gagliardi (present New Jersey commissioner of education).

principal in 1910 while the high school students were still housed at School No.1. She was in charge of the entire school system as well, which, at that time, included just 24 students of high-school age. Ebbert and the students moved into the new Linden High School in 1925, and Ebbert was the Linden High School principal until 1952. In 1967, the school was renamed the Lida M. Ebbert Linden High School in her honor. Following Ebbert's death in 1980, a group of her former students and associates contributed to a fund to perpetuate her memory. Her name, in bronze letters, was placed above the front entrance to the school.

Begun in February 1926, the "continuation school" played an important role in education for almost a decade. The program was first held at School No. 6, and then moved to Soehl Junior High when that school was built, and later went to School No. 8. Students participating in this program spent four days a week employed in industry and one day a week attending school for six hours. On their school day, the students received academic instruction in the morning, and in the afternoon, the boys were taught industrial arts while the girls learned homemaking and child care. Teachers were employed four days a week in the classroom, and the fifth day was devoted to visits to the home and place of employment of every student. Because of changes in state law as a result of the Depression, the continuation school was discontinued in 1933.

School No. 7 was built in 1927, and an addition was constructed in 1929. The school was closed, however, due to a low enrollment of students and repairs that were needed to update the facility. The building was razed and a city park is now located at the site.

The cornerstone for School No. 8 was laid on March 22, 1930 on the site of the home of former mayor H.B Hardenburg, who served in that capacity for 21 years. School No. 8, at 500 West Blancke Street, opened its doors to students in September 1930.

The construction of Deerfield Avenue School No. 9 began in June 1956, and the school opened its doors to students in September 1957. A terra cotta, bold-relief map of the world occupies an entire wall in the lobby. Deerfield is also the site of another Bil Canfield mural. Carol Petusky, named teacher of the year in 1983, commissioned the artist with the $1,000 stipend she received with her award. The mural's presentation brought many dignitaries to the school.

Highland Avenue School No. 10, which also opened on September 9, 1957, was built on a 6-acre parcel of land once owned by the Santo Pietro family and which they, in turn, sold to Simon Kalish in 1950. The City of Linden bought the land from the Sunwood Corporation in 1954.

Joseph E. Soehl Junior High School was built in 1928 and was the only junior high school in Linden until 1957. The front of the building at one time faced Coke Place, with Henry Street on one side, and Elm Street on the other. Additions were constructed in 1958 and 1971, and today the middle school, which occupies an entire block, enrolls students in grades six through eight.

The school known today as Myles J. McManus Middle School was originally built in 1950 as an elementary school. Additions were made to the structure in

LINDEN JUNIOR HIGH SCHOOL, 1932. The school was built in 1928 on Coke Place. It was named Joseph E. Soehl Junior High School on August 22, 1957 in memory of the principal of School No. 3 from 1914 to 1921 and principal of the junior high school from 1928 to 1940. It is currently Joseph E. Soehl Middle School. (Courtesy L. Yeats.)

1958, so that the building could be transformed into a junior high school when Schools No. 9 and 10 were opened in 1957. By 1970, the Linden public school system boasted ten elementary schools, two junior high schools, and one senior high school.

The Linden Board of Education purchased the homestead property of George McGillvray Sr., whose family owned a dairy farm on St. Georges Avenue that extended from Wood Avenue to DeWitt Terrace and as far back as Raritan Road. It was razed in 1971 when the Linden Vocational and Technical building was built on the site across the street from Linden High School. It was considered part of the high school facility. Currently, the building is called the Linden Academy of Science and Technology and is still part of the Linden High School facility.

A plan for a commercial course was drawn up and submitted in May 1916 to the State Department for approval. The program, which was begun in the high school the following year, introduced various branches of science to students, and soon, the curriculum of the high school began to assume some of the characteristics it shows today. Industrial arts, home economics, and art became a part of the Linden public school curriculum around 1914, at which time the board of education appointed one teacher for each subject to teach in the three existing schools. The rapid growth of Linden during the postwar period made it necessary to continually expand educational facilities and increase the teaching personnel in order to provide adequate educational opportunities for Linden youth. Two methods of improving attendance were also adopted during this period—the employment of a school physician and a truant officer. Dr. H. Page of Rahway was the first public school doctor in Linden.

As Linden's curriculum offerings increased, it became necessary to departmentalize the different subject areas so that there was continuity within the school system. In 1925, the first academic subject area to be departmentalized was English.

School nursing, as a service in the Linden public schools, came into being in September 1923. Prior to that time, services of this kind were generalized in nature, functioning under the combined auspices of the local board of health and the state board of health (Bureau of Maternal and Child Health). The board of education, eager to have more nursing services in schools, decided to employ its own nurse. The years between 1923 and 1926 witnessed the rapid growth of the city and, as a result, were busy years for the one school nurse attempting to

MYLES J. MCMANUS JUNIOR HIGH SCHOOL BASEBALL TEAM, 1961. From left to right are (front row) Gregory Martucci, Richie Shannon, Bobby Gall, and Calvin Wheeler; (middle row) Coach Gabe Obester, Michael Testa, Robert Firestone, Ronnie Chase, unidentified, and Coach William Martin; and (back row) Artie Kurek, Buddy Bierman, Mike Long, and Bill Rosenblatt. (Courtesy Steve Yesinko, LBOE.)

function in five schools (which, in short order, became eight schools and a high school). At the September 1927 meeting of the board of education, the school health program and its needs were discussed, resulting in the procurement of another nurse on October 15, 1927. Additional nurses were added to the staff as enrollment grew throughout the city.

Also in 1927, the board of education added the services of a dental clinic to the school system because of the large number of dental defects. The clinic was set up in the centrally located School No. 6. During the Depression, the clinic was opened in the afternoon with dentists serving under the aegis of the Works Progress Administration (WPA). For a time, services were available to both adults and children.

A school optometrist was also soon added to the staff on a part-time basis. One morning a week he examined children brought to him by the school nurse, prescribed glasses, and supplied them at as near to cost as possible. Parents paid for glasses on an installment basis whenever possible. This procedure was later abandoned when the Lions Club began a program to supply needy students with examinations and glasses.

At the same meeting in September 1927, a lively discussion took place on the need for special education to aid disabled children by providing them with classrooms and teachers with specialized training. Two years later, classes for disabled children began at School No. 6. On April 1, 1929, a school psychologist was hired, and that September, a "special education program" for children was initiated. In October 1951, the Department of Special Services was established. The program provided help for students with attendance and speech problems, offering remedial reading and bedside tutoring; the services of a school social worker were also provided. A clinical team to work with emotionally challenged children was approved by the State of New Jersey, at which time a part-time psychiatrist was added to the department's staff.

Student counseling in the early history of Linden's schools, rested chiefly in the hands of homeroom teachers. In 1930, because of the increasing need for guidance, two teachers—a man to work with boys and a woman to work with girls—were appointed as counselors in the junior high school. The results were so beneficial that the board of education decided to extend guidance services to all the public schools. In 1939, a supervisor of guidance was appointed to coordinate this work.

Linden's school lunch program is tied to the history of federal aid. The federal school lunch program began in the 1920s, when American agriculture was burdened with unmarketable surpluses of many farm crops. In the first year of the Depression, the government began buying some of these surpluses to provide a market for farmers and to restore the national economy. This program also helped to supply an adequate diet to needy schoolchildren. The first cafeteria in the Linden public schools was established in the high school on January 5, 1926. Two years later, food service began at the junior high, and in 1929, the first elementary school did the same. By 1944, the food service had increased to six schools and was later extended to include McManus. For several years thereafter, hot food was served in three schools and sandwiches were taken to the schools not having facilities for the preparation of hot food.

Beginning in 1933, Relief and Public Works funds assisted local Parent-Teacher Associations in carrying on local lunch and child feeding programs. Soon the activity gained momentum, and in 1935, Congress authorized the U.S. Department of Agriculture to provide food for lunches. In 1943, Congress authorized the Department of Agriculture to make cash reimbursements to schools that took part in this program. The number of meals served was used as a basis for the distribution of the reimbursement. In 1946, the Federal School Lunch Law was enacted, making federal aid to school lunch programs a permanent national policy with annual appropriations for direct cash grants to states for local programs.

The health and physical education staff was departmentalized in 1924, and in 1953, behind-the-wheel driver's training was included in the program. Sports have always been a big part of the educational program in Linden, but there are two teams wearing the orange and black, in particular, that have made a special mark in local history.

In 1934, the Linden High School football team played nine unscored-upon games against the following teams: Manasquan (18-0), South River (6-0), Rahway (13-0), Thomas Jefferson (12-0), Roselle (9-0), Roselle Park (14-0), Dover (32-0), Hillside (7-0), and Union (12-0). Despite this achievement, the New Jersey Interscholastic Athletic Association declared a three-way tie for the Group III sectional title between Linden, Englewood, and West Orange. Still, the "Coopermen," under Coach Edward Cooper, celebrated by doing a snake dance (like a conga line) up Wood Avenue to a bonfire on the football field.

A few weeks later, on December 28, 1934, the players were honored at a banquet. In a 1987 article in the *News Tribune*, John Deshefy, one of 26 Linden High School football players honored that evening, remembered shuffling on the dance floor in the Linden Elks Club auditorium while Al Kalla and his orchestra played "The Orange and Black." During the banquet, Mayor Myles J. McManus read a statement commending the Tigers for their accomplishment. Plaques were presented to Coach Cooper and Assistant Coach Al Kalla.

At the end of the 1937 season, the Linden High School Class of 1938 saw their boys romp off with the Union County championship and achieve the title of the Group III leaders of North Jersey. The team is best remembered for a game played against undefeated Hillside while Coach Cooper was lying seriously ill in the hospital. In the third quarter, Hillside was leading by a field goal with a score of 10 to 7. Those in the stands rose, and the field resounded with "Fight for Cooper!" The weary but inspired Linden team members fought for their absent coach, and the fans repeated the entreaty. Linden scored, winning 14 to 10. That winning and inspiring season ended on a cold Thanksgiving Day, when the undefeated Linden team beat Union with a score of 20 to 0.

A very active member of his community, Edward R. Cooper was president of the Union County Interscholastic Athletic Association Basketball Committee, and in 1949, he served as president of the New Jersey Board of Approved Basketball Officials. In 1952, he was inducted into the Union County Baseball Hall of Fame. He also served as president of the Linden Lions Club, where he attained perfect attendance for 28 years, and he was a charter member, elder, and trustee of the Linden Presbyterian Church. He received the distinguished award for Union County Interscholastic Athletics in 1980. Cooper served as a football and baseball coach at Linden High School from 1924 to 1946 and as a basketball and track coach from 1925 to 1936. Cooper and his first wife Mildred were the parents of daughters Betty Jane Frazier and Suzanne Voynik, and after Mildred passed away, Cooper married Mary Heller. His family also included stepchildren Guy Heller, Cynthia Hoffman, and Marjore Adler; a sister, Jess Gibbins; and six grandchildren.

William Dougherty said of Coach Cooper, "He brought everyone together." "He was a great coach," Chick Bouska said, "but he was more than a coach. He was like a father, an advisor to all of us. We worked as a team. He kept us together."

1938 Undefeated Football Team. From left to right are (front row) O. Givens, J. Latawiec, F. Kleff, E. Theller, A. Kazary, W. Hausleifer, W. Dougherty, W. Beriont, W. Robinson, and F. MacDuffie; (second row) Coach Edward Cooper, J. Wallace, R. Midgely, R. Fusick, J. Reichardf, F. Fonda, R. Dalziel, R. Diduk, T. Dooley, J. Alber, and Mr. Deufsch; (third row) Coach Goodwin, F. Pirrocco, J. Klufkowski, E. Kasmin, W. Swanson, J. Mulhall, J. Leili, E. Bolfon, E. Spader, and I. Gutkin; and (fourth row) D. Campeau, W. Fecho, J. Butchko, W. Fullerton, and B. Cooper. (Courtesy LBOE.)

LINDEN HIGH SCHOOL GRADUATION. From left to right are Principal Edward Cooper; Elmer Ruth, president of the Linden Board of Education; Vincent Paul David; and Superintendent of Schools Emanuel Bedrick. (Courtesy Allen Bedrick.)

Six boys in the Givens family—Jackson, Nathaniel ("Noonie"), Ulysses ("Lis"), Freddy, "Rosie," and Oscar—played several sports, including football, for Cooper from 1925 to 1940 at Linden High School. "I think I might have been the first coach in the state to coach six brothers from the same family," Cooper said with a smile as wide as a proud father. "They were all great young men."

The Linden home field was named Edward R. Cooper Athletic Field in honor of Coach Cooper. This honor, along with the naming of the John L. Beriont Field House after a 1934 graduate of Linden High School who was a patent lawyer and served as a major in the Army Air Corps during World War II, were celebrated on October 7, 1967, during the halftime of the Linden-Rahway game. Coincidentally, the board of education president at that time was Elmer Ruth, the quarterback of the 1934 team. Cooper was a regular visitor to the field named for him after his retirement and up until his death on April 6, 1988 at the age of 85.

Linden superintendents have guided the school system through many challenges and changes since the early days of education in Linden, as the following brief descriptions illustrate.

D.A. Howell (1907–1935) was an 1896 graduate of Trenton Normal School and received a degree from New York University in 1916. He became head of the local schools in 1907, coming from Pompton Lakes to Linden's solitary school on East Linden Avenue. When this school burned down in 1909, the first of the modern schools (School No. 1) was built as a combined grammar and high school. Under Howell's direction, the school system grew to eight grammar schools, a junior high school, and a senior high school. He saw the student population increase from a high school graduating class of just 4 pupils to 170. After spending 42 years in the teaching profession, 28 of which were as chief of the local system, Howell resigned in 1935 and retired to his farm in Newton, New Jersey.

Paul R. Brown (1935–1957) received his first degree (doctor of arts) at Simpson College of Indianapolis. He also had a bachelor's degree from Boston University, a master's degree in education from Columbia University, and a master's degree in supervision and administration from Rutgers University. He received his doctorate in education from Rutgers in 1936, and his first teaching post put him in St. George, Delaware as teaching principal. In 1935, Brown was selected from a group of 72 applicants for the superintendent of schools position in Linden to succeed D.A. Howell. The office became one of added responsibility with the official awarding of a second-class rating to the local schools and their severance from the county as an independent system. Brown resigned the post in June 1957 after 22 years as superintendent.

Emanuel Bedrick (1957–1967) was educated in New York City and later graduated from Dickinson High School, Jersey City. He received a bachelor of arts and a master's degree from New York University. In 1927, he became a practice teacher in the junior high, following that up in 1929 with a position as teacher of history and social studies at Linden High School. In 1940, Bedrick transferred to the senior high school to teach citizenship. On February 1, 1944, he became teaching principal of School No. 7, and in July of 1946 transferred to School No. 5 as principal. In March of 1952, he was appointed acting principal of the junior high school but never served in that capacity because in August 1952, the board of education appointed him the first general supervisor of instruction for the Linden public school system. May 1953 marked his appointment as assistant superintendent of Linden public schools—the new title for that position. In June 1957, Bedrick became superintendent of Linden public schools. During his tenure as superintendent, School No. 9, School No. 10 and School No. 4 Annex were constructed. Additions were completed to School No. 2, School No. 5, School No. 6, McManus, and Soehl. Renovations to the high school, with its new science wing and gymnasium, were completed and administrative offices were set up in the house on the site of the present-day Linden Academy of Science and Technology building. At that time, plans were developed for the site to become an area vocational-technical school. Bedrick died on November 30, 1967.

Dr. James O'Brien (1968–1971) attended Elizabeth public schools. He received his bachelor's degree from the University of Newark in 1936 and earned a master's degree from Rutgers University. In May 1940, he became the Linden schools' director of guidance, though in 1943 he entered the U.S. Navy. In September 1945, the title of director was changed to supervisor of guidance and special services, and O'Brien resumed the job in 1946 after returning home. In 1951, O'Brien earned his doctor of education degree from Rutgers University.

That same year, he was appointed vice principal of the junior high school (now Soehl Middle School) and promoted to principal a year later. In 1956, he was given an additional special assignment to serve as the coordinator of junior high school activities in the $3.5 million school expansion program.

Americo R. Taranto (1972–1985) was educated in Linden public schools, received his bachelor's degree from Lebanon Valley College, and his master's degree from Rutgers University. He also completed graduate studies at Rutgers, New York University, and Upsala College. Taranto's first job with the school system was teaching at Linden High School; however, shortly after he began, World War II interrupted his career and he gave three years of military service. Taranto returned to teaching after the war and, in 1949, changed direction to become an assistant school psychologist in the district's special services department. In 1957, Taranto moved up to the post of school psychologist, and soon after was promoted to the department's assistant directorship. In 1963, Taranto was given an added responsibility when he was made principal of School No. 7. He held the two positions concurrently until 1966, when his role changed again. This time he was entrusted with the leadership of two elementary schools—School No. 7 and School No. 2. Taranto later rose to the position of assistant superintendent, and in July 1972 was appointed superintendent. During his tenure as superintendent, academic standards were being lowered nationally. However, Taranto held fast to the high level of expectation established by the Linden tradition. He stimulated academic achievement by setting a stringent district-wide homework policy and by developing rigorous attendance and graduation requirements. He expanded the district's reading program and made writing a top priority. He supported many new programs, including the preschool program for handicapped children, Targeting and Evaluating Developmentally Delayed Youngsters (TEDDY). He also supported a vocational training and job-placement program for handicapped students at the high school level. He was also involved in the development of the district's vocational school by establishing the program and developing the curriculum.

Thomas W. Long (1986–1992) received a bachelor of science degree from East Stroudsburg University in 1951 and a master of education degree from Rutgers University in 1957. He also received 50 additional graduate credits from Rutgers and Kean College of New Jersey. Long began his career as a teacher at Linden High School in 1951. He was appointed vice principal of McManus Junior High School in 1963 and held that position until 1969. He was then appointed principal of Joseph E. Soehl Junior High School in 1969 and principal of McManus Junior High School in 1971. Long was the assistant superintendent from 1972 until 1985, and in 1986 was appointed superintendent, a position he held until his retirement in 1992. During his tenure as superintendent, Long introduced the pre-school program for four-year-old children, the Naval ROTC program, full-time nurses on the elementary level, an elementary guidance counselor, and the expansion of the elementary science program. In conjunction with the Linden Police Department, Long also introduced the DARE program. Additionally, he

SCHOOL OFFICIALS. Mrs. Modashal was supervisor of special education in Linden Public Schools. Americo R. Taranto was superintendent of schools from 1972 to 1985. (Courtesy Frank Taranto.)

established a strong partnership with local industry, including Merck and Exxon, and assisted in the renovation of School No. 5 and School No. 6.

James B. Clarke Jr. (1992–1999) graduated from Springfield College in 1957 with a bachelor of science degree in teacher education, physical education, and biology, and he received his master's degree in guidance and psychological services in 1967. Clarke taught biology and physical education and was a guidance counselor in the Poughkeepsie, New York school system from 1957 to 1971. He was appointed principal of School No. 8 in Poughkeepsie in 1971 and held that position until 1980. Clarke worked as an associate superintendent from 1980 to 1982 and served as interim superintendent during the 1982–1983 school year. He was appointed superintendent of the Poughkeepsie City School District in 1983 and held that position until 1989. From 1989 to 1992, Clarke was district superintendent for Saratoga County, one of 41 positions in New York State. He was appointed superintendent of schools in Linden in 1992 and was instrumental in changing the focus and name of the Vocational School to the Linden Academy of Science and Technology, as well as ensuring that every third-, fourth-, and fifth-grade classroom within the district had at least one bank of four computers. He also instituted computer labs and technology labs at the middle schools; TV and Technology Labs at Linden High School; Research Centers in the middle schools and high school, and the district became involved in the Merck Institute of

Science Education. Currently, Clarke is the interim superintendent at Hudson City School District in New York.

Joseph E. Martino (2000–present) received a bachelor of science degree from East Stroudsburg University in 1972 and a master of arts education degree from College of New Jersey University. He earned an administration certificate at Kean University of New Jersey and studied at Columbia and Harvard Universities. Martino began his career as a teacher of physical education and driver education at Linden High School in 1961, but left the city in 1965 to be a teacher and coach in Colonia, New Jersey. In 1977–1978, Martino was an administrator and coach at Rahway, New Jersey, and he came back to Linden as an administrator and a coach in 1979. The team won the football championship in 1983. He was the director of Health, Physical Education, Safety, Athletic Medical Services 1983–1991. During 1991–1992 he was the interim principal at Linden High School. In 1993 he became the high school principal. He was appointed superintendent of schools in 1999. During his tenure as superintendent, Martino has been instrumental in developing the international baccalaureate degree program in Linden schools and a partnership program to help develop corporate and community support of Linden schools. Due to increased student enrollment, Martino is overseeing the School No. 4 Annex addition. At its completion, the

COACHES OF 1963 SEASON (CLASS OF 1964) FOOTBALL TEAM. From left to right are Paul Blue, who retired in June 2001 after a 44-year teaching and coaching career in Linden; Joseph Martino, who in 2000 became Linden's superintendent of schools; William Martin; and Peter O'Halloran. (Courtesy LBOE.)

facility will no longer be referred to as School No. 4 Annex but School No. 4 Dill Avenue.

Parochial schools also played a part in educating the youth of Linden. St. Elizabeth of Hungary Elementary School officially opened on September 12, 1927, for 120 students. Three sisters of the Dominican order formed the nucleus of the faculty, each teaching two grades a curriculum that included religion, arithmetic, reading, spelling, geography, history, music, and art. The school consisted of eight classrooms and an auditorium. By 1929, the eight grades each had teachers, and in 1943, a kindergarten was started. Three years later, to accommodate increased enrollment, the pastor converted the auditorium into additional classrooms. An addition was constructed in 1947. The Home-School Association was instituted in 1957.

The groundbreaking for St. Theresa of the Child Jesus School took place on June 27, 1926, and in September 1930, the new grammar school opened its classrooms to the children of the parish. The first class, containing 15 students, graduated from the school in June 1933. To provide eating facilities for the schoolchildren and the sisters, a cafeteria was built, with the work completed on April 2, 1962. On February 10, 1963, a school library opened its doors with 2,575 volumes and many visual aids.

In 1950, St. John the Apostle School opened under the direction of the first principal, Sister Mary Adele, with 696 students. The location of St. John's Church and school, which are housed in one building, is unique, as it is situated in the township of Clark and in the city of Linden (its official address is Valley Road in Clark). With rapid increases in enrollment, the school required more space and the construction of a third story soon became necessary. On March 11, 1952, work was underway to add 22 classrooms. The original student body was under the care and direction of 11 teaching sisters of St. Dominic of Caldwell, New Jersey; 3 lay teachers; and the principal. In 1961, the staff included 19 teaching sisters and 10 lay teachers. Since the 1970s, St. John the Apostle School has offered a kindergarten program; it now offers two full-day kindergarten classes.

9. THE CHRISTIAN COMMUNITY

In a history written by the Reformed Church of Linden for its 100th anniversary program, entries in the diary of Meeker Wood are quoted: "Sunday—attended church at Rahway in the morning and Elizabeth in the afternoon." Research of the area further back in time shows Union County was a part of the extensive area originally possessed by the Netherlanders and called New Belgium. Later, it was known as New Netherlands. Achter Kol (now strangely corrupted into "Arthur Kill") and Kill van Kull gave their names to the adjacent waters separating New Jersey and Staten Island.

Immediately after the British seizure of New Netherlands in 1664, however, the English commander and first governor Colonel Richard Nicolls made grants of land to a number of English Puritan families who came from Connecticut and made Elizabethtown the first permanent English settlement in New Jersey. All of the early residents of Elizabethtown, except the 30 colonists and servants brought to the New World by Sir Philip Carteret on *The Philip*, were Puritans or Congregationalists. Carteret's people were Roman Catholics and Anglicans. When the first legislature of the colony met at Elizabethtown in 1668, the great majority of its members were representatives of English Puritans.

After Sir George Carteret the royal proprietor died in 1779, William Penn and 11 others, all Quakers, purchased the title from Carteret's heirs in 1782. Robert Barclay was then made governor and numerous Scots, including both Quakers and Presbyterians, followed him and made important settlements such as the historically significant Scotch Plains, New Jersey. Many Scottish colonists came because of the religious strife in their native country.

For two centuries, Quakers were very influential in the political and educational affairs of New Jersey. The Quakers were always motivated by three basic ideals: piety, practicality, and philanthropy. They did not require higher education for a ministry, but depended on what they called "the inner light." Their yearly, monthly, and quarterly meetings knit them into a well-functioning unit.

Religious strife in France, also, following the Revocation of the Edict of Nantes, caused many Huguenots (French Presbyterians) to settle at Elizabethtown. Among them were the families of Noe, Traubles (Tremley), and Boudinot, which a little later gave to the United States the illustrious Elias Boudinot, president of the continental congress and founder of the American Bible Society.

From 1665 to 1740, when Elizabethtown was incorporated as the Borough of Elizabeth, education was chiefly a church function, customarily conducted by the Presbyterian minister as no Catholic, Episcopalian, or Quaker schools were opened between those dates. The Episcopalian minister provided catechetical instruction to the children of his congregation while the Quakers emphasized home instruction. The few Catholics probably arranged with visiting priests for instruction in their faith. Education was thus of a religious nature, though among the Presbyterians and Quakers vocational goals were included.

The first house of worship in this settlement was the First Presbyterian Church on Broad Street, which was built in 1665 as a plain wooden structure also used for meetings of the Supreme Court, General Assembly, and the legislature, as Elizabethtown was the first capital of New Jersey. A new church was erected in 1724 and enlarged in 1766 with a bell, steeple, clock, and spire. On the night of January 25, 1780, a party of British troops and refugees, numbering nearly 400, crossed on the ice from Staten Island to Trembly's Point and were led by three Elizabethtown Tories by the nearest and most retired route to the town. Here they secured a few prisoners, robbed many residents, burned the courthouse and meeting house, and retreated with haste by way of De Hart's Point without loss. Washington spoke of this event a day or two after as "the late misfortune and

WATERMARK FROM ELIZABETHTOWN BOOK, C. 1736. The book was discovered after the press conference on February 26, 2001. The mark shows a crest with Elizabeth. Amazing!

GRACE EPISCOPAL CHURCH. The first marriage to take place in the church was that of Fred Blancke and Isabel Langley. The building was razed in 1968. The congregation's current home is on De Witt Terrace. (Courtesy L. Yeats.)

disgrace of Elizabeth Town." At the time of the American Revolution, the Presbyterian clergymen influenced their congregations to support the rebel cause, with subsequent British retaliation in the destruction of church property; thus the church was burned by the British in 1780.

The College of New Jersey, an old academy that stood where the lecture-room of the First Presbyterian Church now stands, and which was also burned down during the Revolution, contained the first recitation-rooms of what is now Princeton University. The present structure was completed in 1789 and the chapel added in 1864.

Presbyterian minister Dr. Kempshall, in his historical discourse delivered January 25, 1880 celebrating the Centennial Anniversary of the burning of the church, said the following:

> The lot on which the church was built included burying-ground. Graves were sometimes dug under the floor of the church, a custom familiar to the early settlers like ancestors in England, so that nearly the whole area of this 1724 church, is probably occupied with the dust which awaits the archangel's trump, of the first two or three generations of the people of the town.

Some of the headstones, removed to give room for the additions to the church, were set in the walls, where they can still be seen. Among them are two old headstones bearing the date 1687, erected to the memory of two sons of the widow of a Captain Lawrence, who married Governor Philip Carteret as her second husband. In 1762, immediately after the settlement of Reverend James Caldwell, it was voted by the trustees that the burial ground be enclosed with a fence. In this old churchyard lie forefathers of Elizabethtown and many others, such as Jonathan Dickinson, Dr. John McDowell, Reverend James Caldwell, Honorable Elias Boudinot, Robert Ogden, First General Matthias Ogden, Governor Aaron Ogden, Dr. Nicholas Murray, and Shepard Kollock. According to the Newmark-Weisbrodt Manuscript of Linden, the following familiar names of the Linden area supported this church: James Hinds, Moses Thompson, Robert Moss, Aaron Thompson, John Winans, John Hinds, Jonas Wood, William Oliver, Ebenezer Spinning, Joseph Halsey, Joseph Frazee, and Charles Tooker Jr.

The Second Presbyterian congregation was founded in 1820 as a separation from the First Presbyterian Church, which had become overcrowded. The church building was constructed a year later. Graves at the rear of the church were eventually removed to Evergreen Cemetery in Hillside, New Jersey.

The next oldest congregation of Elizabethtown was Saint John's Episcopal Church at 61 Broad Street, organized in 1704. In 1706, the foundation of the building was laid on ground given by Colonel Richard Townley. In this churchyard are buried many of the earliest inhabitants of Elizabethtown. The clergy of this denomination supported the Tory cause during the War for Independence with the result that local rebels destroyed the social structure and property of the congregation.

The Methodists influenced the borough through the introduction of circuit-riding preachers, yearly revivals, preachers, and adult classes under the clerical and lay leadership. They followed a policy of cooperating with nondenominational service units. This denomination also established a separate congregation for African Americans. One Methodist congregation was the only church of the borough that permitted women to hold an executive office in church government. The Methodist church was first organized in 1785. The Reverend Thomas Morrell, one of the fathers of the Methodist church in America, preached for many years at Elizabethtown. He was also a major in the Revolutionary army.

The Baptists advanced in the borough the goals of the humanitarian movement through state societies and regional groups. They especially emphasized support of the missions. The role of the Roman Catholic denomination came as late as 1858 when Saint Patrick's Parish was established.

As the population of the Rahway area increased, settlers wanted a church local to their homes as it was difficult to travel outside the settlement and worse during inclement weather. The Presbyterians had been making the long walk to Elizabethtown for many years and finally, just prior to the "Hard Winter" of 1741, the Elizabethtown congregation began sending their ministers to preach in the homes and barns of the Rahway members. Alex and Robin Shipley in *Rediscover*

Rahway state that Reverend Jonathan Dickinson of the First Presbyterian Church and a Mr. Vaun, the Episcopal minister from Elizabethtown, often led services in a barn on St. Georges Avenue. That winter, the congregation experienced a season so unbearably cold that the journey to Elizabethtown became almost impossible. It was during this winter that Reverend Dickinson helped to organize the first Presbyterian Church in the Rahway area. The construction of the church commenced in 1741 and was completed within the next year. The Shipleys state:

> It was built near the bend in the main driveway of the Rahway Cemetery. The cemetery, which became the church's burial ground, contains many eighteenth century headstones that are still in fine condition. Grave markers which stood on the north, south and west sides of the church clearly outline its position.

The church membership was made up of New Englanders, Scottish Presbyterians, persons of Irish and Welsh extraction, Puritans, Covenanters, and Quakers. The Revolutionary War brought hardships and loss of life to the church as the British considered a Presbyterian and a rebel to be one and the same.

> A Presbyterian patriot who was continually harassed by the British was Abraham Clark, signer of the Declaration of Independence. The Clark family burial plot, located in the church's cemetery, lends evidence to the belief that Clark was a member of the Rahway church.

As stated earlier, Christians living in 1861 Linden Township would travel on foot and by horse to both Rahway and Elizabeth to attend church services each Sunday. People attended for two hours in the morning and two hours in the afternoon.

Finally, in 1866, the settlers of Linden came together to establish a Sabbath school for all those of the Christian denominations through the efforts of the Presbyterian Church. By 1866, a Methodist faction began under the leadership of Sanford Stimpson. These meetings were called Union Meetings. They continued harmoniously until 1869, when an Episcopal group was introduced into the community. A petition was circulated among the landowners seeking direction as to which denomination would be favored in the settlement. Before a decision could be reached by the committee, Stimpson proceeded to hire a Methodist and a Presbyterian clergyman to lead the morning services, a decision which was met with disfavor.

In the early days, when an Episcopal group came to the community, the faction invited a Reverend Earl to conduct services, and he moved his people to the Linden Hotel. Ferdinand Blancke, a large landholder and a great influence in the Linden community, was contacted for advice and a committee was formed from the remaining denominations. They were advised to seek out the Dutch Reformed Church. In 1869, money was promised by the Board of Missions of the

METHODIST EPISCOPAL CHURCH, WINTER 1924. This building was once the Stiles schoolhouse. It was physically moved to its present location on North Wood Avenue. The original building was somewhat remodeled and is currently the Linden Methodist Church. (Courtesy Shirley Stuewe.)

Dutch Reformed Church in North America to establish a church in Linden. A meeting was called for all interested parties in the fall of that year. A society was formed, a board of trustees elected, and services established in the schoolhouse under the leadership of a Reverend J. Lockwood, a Congregationalist. On May 10, 1871, the Linden Reformed Church was organized with 11 charter members. The certificate of incorporation was filed on July 4, 1871.

Ferdinand Blancke deeded property at the corner of Wood Avenue and Henry Street to the church, and on Christmas Day 1871, the new building was dedicated. The evening festivities surrounded the church's first wedding, of Mr. and Mrs. William Wood. According to the Newmark-Weisbrot WPA manuscript, the church property was enclosed with a fence, and 12 horse sheds were built at the rear of the church. These sheds remained until 1909. Reverend Oscar Gesner served from 1871 to 1873, during which time attendance at the services was sometimes as high as 150 people. Soon, however, the Methodists and Episcopalians broke ties and left the struggling church. The Presbyterians held up letters of transfer, hoping to pressure the newly formed group into the Presbyterian denomination. Reverend Gesner resigned shortly after, though he did remain as a member of pulpit supply for the next 20 years. In 1880, Ferdinand Blancke assumed the mortgage payments, and in 1891, he deeded the property on the corner of Wood Avenue and Gesner Street for a parsonage. In 1914, Reverend

Albertus Van Raalte was installed as pastor. Reverend William Schmitz became minister in 1917.

Reverend A. Burkhardt followed as minister until 1926 and was himself followed by another young minister, Reverend Alvin Langwith, who stayed until 1932. The church was without an installed minister for the next five years. Dr. E.H. Gelvin, who was serving a small Congregational group in Tremley Point, followed. He was given a small salary and the use of the manse. He continued his ministry at the Reformed Church until 1936. Reverend Herbert Schneider came in 1937 and ushered in one of the most productive periods in the church's history. During this time, the Hungarian Calvinists used the sanctuary for services as well. Schneider resigned in March 1943. Reverend Forest Decker arrived and the upward trend continued. Servicemen were returning from World War II; the church school flourished. Old debts were paid. The choir loft was enlarged. A new organ and stained-glass windows were installed, both gifts of Sadie and Fred Wood. A great deal of effort by many people allowed the burning of the mortgage in 1959.

In the spring of 1969, a campaign was started to renovate Wood Hall. A new organ was purchased. The Sadie Wood Fund was established to loan money to any of our young people planning on entering the ministry.

BOY SCOUT TROOP 34. *This troop was sponsored by the Reformed Church. From left to right are (front row) Davison, Sauer, Tevlin, Sauer, Morrison, Palermo, Johnstone, Hodges, unidentified, Maclean, and unidentified; (middle row) Christophers, Blancke, Moody, Metro, Shields, Moritz, White, Nelson, Hoffman, Little, Hales, Serra, and Segesser; and (back row) McClosky, unidentified, Hayden, Andersen, unidentified, Kiseli, Ebel, Berkenstock, Hunter, Christophers, Angelback, and Hill. (Courtesy Al Palermo.)*

Before the incorporation of the Methodist church in the city of Linden in 1866, Methodist societies met at various private homes and shared a pastor with the First Church in Rahway. At the suggestion of the Newark Annual Conference, these groups became legally incorporated as the Linden Methodist Episcopal Church, and on September 25, 1866, the official certificate was signed by Sanford Stimpson, Henry D. Ralph, John Clay, Elizal A. Tucker, and Cornelius Leveridge. It was filed in the Union County clerk's office on September 28, 1866.

In 1873, $250 was paid to Ferdinand Blancke as partial payment on the purchase of an old schoolhouse and a mortgage for $1,000 was executed. The building, located on North Stiles Street, was repaired and fitted for church use. It was heated by a wood-burning stove and lighted by oil lamps. An 80-foot-by-125-foot lot was deeded to the First Methodist Episcopal Church of Linden by Caroline and Ferdinand Blancke and on July 25, 1881, the building was moved to its present location and improved. The first full-time pastor, Reverend S.P. Lacey, was appointed in 1889. On September 28, 1907, the congregation held a groundbreaking ceremony for a new parsonage in the church and an extension to the church building.

The parsonage was completed in 1908. In 1911, Reverend A.G. Schatzman organized the first Boy Scout troop. In 1916, a kitchen was added to the church building, and the church was wired for electricity (the parsonage, however, was not wired for another nine years). In 1917, the Home Guard was given permission to use the church's gymnasium. In 1921, the church purchased the property next to the parsonage and it was decided to replace the church with a larger one. The laying of the new cornerstone was held on Sunday, September 20, 1925. A mortgage was taken over by C.H. Winans. Despite the hard financial times of the late 1920s and early 1930s, the church continued to grow. The Ladies Aid managed to keep paying interest on the mortgage for eight years. In 1939, the official name of the church was changed to the Methodist Church of Linden. The mortgage was at last paid off in 1947. A two-story addition was completed in1963.

Grace Episcopal Church traces its beginnings to a small group of Episcopalians that met in the home of A. Wheeler. Reverend Dr. J. Abercrombie of Rahway presided. He also led the first services of the Episopal Church in Linden on Sunday, April 3, 1870 in the little schoolhouse on Stiles Street, which was rented from the Linden School Association. A church building was started in 1873 on a lot on West Linden Avenue donated by Meeker Wood. On January 31, 1874, the Episcopal Society of Linden was incorporated as the Trustees of Grace Episcopal Church of Linden. Members assembled at the home of Meeker Wood, where Reverend John Denniston presided over services until 1875, when the church building was completed. However in April 1876, the church and lot were sold at the sheriff's sale, and purchased back in 1877 by the congregation under the leadership of Walther Luttgens. In September 1887, the building was moved to the corner of Washington Avenue and Elm Street, on a plot donated by Luttgens. In 1886, the church was incorporated under state law as The Rector, Wardens, and Vestrymen of Grace Episcopal Church in Linden.

About a year later, the parishioners became dissatisfied with the location of the building since many of them lived on the north side of the railroad tracks. Walther Luttgens offered a lot at the corner of Washington Avenue and Elm Street, and the church was moved in September 1887. This was planned and accomplished in the early morning to get the structure across the railroad tracks before the trains were scheduled to run. Grace Church attained status as a full-fledged parish in 1941, and merged with Saint Andrew's Mission in 1967. The property at Washington Avenue and Elm Street was sold, the building razed, and the congregation moved to the Mission building at DeWitt Terrace and Robbinwood Terrace.

Saint Andrew's Episcopal Church began in 1952 to meet the need for an Episcopal church in Linden's Sunnyside section. Reverend Hugh Morton (rector of Grace Church at the time) held the first service of the new mission dedicated to Saint Andrew in the McManus School music room on March 2, 1952. This room was used as a temporary chapel for two years. The first service held in the new church building at DeWitt and Robbinwood Terraces was the midnight eucharist on Christmas Eve 1954, and the first vicar was Reverend Joseph DiRaddo. About this time, Saint Andrew's ceased being a Mission Chapel of Grace Church and became a Diocesan Mission. In 1965, discussions between the two congregations began concerning a possible merger of the two congregations, culminating with the merger in 1967. Because Grace Church was already incorporated under state law, Saint Andrew's was absorbed into Grace. The first rector of the combined congregations was the Reverend Charles Cesaretti. Since then, the church building was completely renovated c. 1980 and an addition, called St. Andrew's Hall, was built in the early 1990s. A new rectory was built on the Melrose Terrace side of the property in the early 1980s. In 2001, the parish entered into a "shared ministry" arrangement with Saint Luke's Episcopal Church of Roselle. Separate services and facilities continue to be maintained, but both parishes share the services of the Reverend Terence Blackburn as rector.

In 1861, Linden Township encompassed a larger area, including what is now Roselle. The First Presbyterian Church of Roselle began on June 12, 1868 in a little schoolhouse just west of the Walnut Street Bridge. Thirty-six persons united in membership under a covenant. John Seaton and Aaron D. Hope were elders. Trustees were David Mulford, Aaron W. Smith, N.D. Sticrer, Rezeau Brown, William S. Williams, Aaron Clark II, and John W. Mulford. Mulford also erected the church building. In time, a west wing was added. The cornerstone was laid in September of 1868. Edison's electric lights were introduced and it was the first church in the world to be lighted.

The Baptist church was an organization in Roselle that grew out of a union Sabbath school that met at Wheatsheaf. Accordingly, in June of 1870, the Baptist Bible school was organized with 19 members.

The history of the denomination of the African Methodist Episcopal (AME) Church began in 1787. The Grier Avenue Methodist Church held services at 60 Grier Avenue in the early 1920s in Linden Township, in what was then the Greater Elizabeth section. Except for this notation, no other documentation can be found about the church. In 1927, the site was rented to the African Methodist Episcopal Church. In 1930 the group was led by the Reverend J. Clark of New Brunswick. In 1932 it was known as Allen Chapel, AME Church. The Reverend Jacob N. Washington served the congregation for several years. The pastor in 1937 was the Reverend S.A. Gatlin. A current AME church in Linden is the Antioch AME Zion Church at 900 Baltimore Avenue.

First Baptist Church was founded in 1922 by a group consisting of the Harvey, Samson, Johnson, and Read families. It was founded at the residence of Herman Johnson. Services were then held in School No. 4. The location of 1301 Lincoln Street was purchased in 1924. At the time the church was erected in 1926, there were only 30 members. Various ministers served for short periods of time until 1940 when Reverend S.E. Schell Jr. became pastor. Under his guidance, the building was renovated and enlarged to meet the needs of a large and growing membership. Reverend Lewis Steele is the current pastor.

In 1927, trustees of the Elizabeth Presbytery purchased a plot of ground in the City of Linden with the hope of erecting a church thereon in the future. The site, located in a development known as Sunnyside Gardens, was to be the future home of Linden Presbyterian Church. During 1936, the Second Presbyterian

SAINT GEORGE BYZANTINE CATHOLIC CHURCH. Their mortgage was paid off mostly from the sales of all of the pirogis made by these dedicated women. They are lovingly called the Pirohi Ladies. From left to right are the Mrs. Durin, Bigan, Hrekovik, Kuchna, Valiga, Gelles, Father George Billy, Mrs. Krupa, Seamon, Tkach, Bachkovsky, Yacik, Rebovchik, Turnitsa, Halajchik, Andricik, Sisak, Mitrik, and Semko. (Courtesy Mary Kuhtik.)

95

REVEREND KENNETH WALTER. The reverend is setting the cornerstone of the Linden Presbyterian Church's addition of the church school in 1957.

Church of Elizabeth secured permission from the Presbytery to start a mission in Linden. Meetings were held in a little building known as the Suburban Club in the Berlant Park area of Linden, near Raritan Road, but were discontinued after two years. During October 1939, the Presbytery secured the services of James L. Ewalt and William H. Felmeth, students at the Princeton Theological Seminary, to make a second attempt at starting a mission church. The first meeting was held on November 5, 1939 at the Skating House in Woodrow Wilson Park with 34 persons present. This new organization was called the Linden Community Chapel. In July 1940, work was begun on a building at the corner of Princeton Road and Orchard Terrace, which was dedicated February 2, 1941. On March 11, 1941, the Linden Presbyterian Church was formally organized. Reverend James L. Ewalt was installed as first pastor on May 2, 1941. Ewalt was called to enter the military chaplaincy, and dissolved the pastoral relationship on May 4, 1943. The Reverend Kenneth E. Walter was extended a unanimous call and installed on November 16, 1943, at which time a manse was purchased for his use. In March of 1951, the new Sanctuary Unit was dedicated. The church's physical expansion was completed with the dedication of the Church School Building on March 2, 1958. In 1963, the membership of the church was almost 800. This led to the calling of an assistant pastor, the Reverend Tony M. MacNaughton, who was installed on September 10, 1967. In March of 1971, he was called to be pastor of the Hilldale Park Church. The Reverend Kenneth E. Walter answered the

Master's final call on Memorial Day, May 30, 1978. On September 19, 1979 Rev. Dr. William C. Weaver was installed, becoming the third and present pastor to serve this congregation.

Calvin Presbyterian Church has its origin dating back to 1913, when people from Slovakia joined the wave of immigrants coming to the United States from eastern Europe. Many gathered for worship at the Reformed Hungarian Church in Perth Amboy until 1924 when the Slovak people purchased a property on Herbert Street in Perth Amboy. They remained there for several years until the Slovaks living in Fords and Linden were able to both start congregations in their respective communities.

On March 24, 1934, two lots on Arthur Street were purchased from Florence Roe for the building of a Slovak Presbyterian Church and a congregation of 80 charter members gathered faithfully for worship. At first, all worship services were in Slovak, but as families grew and non-Slovak people were attracted to the church, the congregation recognized a need for English language services and new members. The congregation in Linden thus became bilingual and continues in this special ministry to this day. There are two services of worship every Sunday, one in English and one in Slovak, followed by church school for children and youth. Calvin Presbyterian Church is well known for its Hand-bell Choirs, of which they currently have three.

The Linden Assembly of God was incorporated in 1933 as the Polish Pentecostal Full Gospel Church. Its founder and first pastor was Reverend N. Stecewicz of Newark. The first meetings were held in the home of the J. Guznik family, and were known as cottage meetings. In October 1934, land was acquired at 416 Bower Street to build a new church. Reverend John Midura of New York City was the pastor. The men of the congregation built the church themselves. The first service was held in an unfinished building on Christmas 1934. In the year 1953, the name was changed to Linden Assembly of God.

The congregation of the Magyar Reformed Church was organized by Pastor Reverend L. Hunyady. On December 7, 1952, the church was formally chartered. The name was chosen to document the freedom of worship in the land of the free. Services were first held in the building of the Hungarian Round Table Charity Association on Maple Avenue. A building was purchased early in 1953 at 1135 Clark Street with the official dedication on September 27, 1953.

First Pentecostal Church began when the Reverend Mabel L. Bullock began holding services in the home of Louise Walker on East 19th Street in 1954. Soon the "parlor church" was outgrown. The former synagogue on East 18th Street was purchased in 1959. The name was changed to the Zion Temple of the First Pentecostal Church of America. The Right Reverend Mabel L. Bullock had been elevated to the position of bishop. Bishop Geanette Leach is the current pastor.

On October 10, 1948, an army chapel was purchased from Camp Shanks, New York for the Church of Christ in Linden. It was disassembled and then reassembled at North Stiles Street and Raritan Road. Many of the original nails were straightened and reused. It is now the site of a private family residence.

Saint Elizabeth Roman Catholic Church began in 1895, when William McDonagh of Linden applied to the bishop for permission to build a Catholic Church in Linden. There were only 14 families interested at the time, so permission was denied. In the meantime, however, mass was celebrated on Sundays at the McDonagh home, located at the corner of Blancke Street and Washington Avenue. Some years later on Blancke Street, near where the police headquarters is today, a realty office was turned into the first home of the congregation on May 2, 1909. A mission was started by the Franciscan Fathers of New York City. Reverend Francis Koch was the first resident priest. The mission was transferred to the Benedictine Fathers of Newark on August 26, 1910 with Reverend Meinrad Hettinger as pastor. However, the Catholic residents represented 11 different nationalities and preferred their own priests even if this necessitated traveling to Elizabeth or Rahway. Father Hettinger worked with the children of these people and welded them together to form a congregation for Saint Elizabeth. When he came to Linden, he lived in the converted realty office.

The cornerstone for the new Saint Elizabeth's Church was laid on the feast of Our Lady of Sorrows, September 15, 1912. The first mass in the new church was celebrated by Father Hettinger on November 19, 1922, which was appropriately the Feast of Saint Elizabeth. In that same month, Father Hettinger initiated plans for the construction of a new rectory, which was completed by November 21, 1915. On Thanksgiving Day, 1926, ground was broken for the present Saint Elizabeth's School. In August 1927, the Sisters of Saint Dominic moved into a newly-acquired two-family house on Hussa Street and classes began in the new school in September 1927. Six grades constituted the first enrollment, and June 1930 saw its first graduating class. In 1932, Father Hettinger died. In January 1933, Reverend Gabriel Steines was appointed; he died on September 2, 1941. Reverend Walter Lee became the administrator of Saint Elizabeth's late in 1941. In 1943, he was appointed pastor. Father Walter concluded his term as pastor in June 1944. In the same month, Reverend Louis Seiser was appointed pastor. In 1947, ground was broken for an addition to the school and in 1950, the new church ground was broken. The first mass was celebrated in the church in 1952.

St. George Byzantine Catholic Church began in 1922, when 17 Slavish Catholic families of the Greek rite gathered together for the purpose of organizing a church in Linden. The founding fathers, who purchased property collectively, signed a bank note in order to obtain a mortgage for $10,000. Once the loan was procured, everyone pitched in to help. The church was completed and dedicated in 1923, and Father Peter Kustan from Saint John the Baptist Greek Catholic Church of Rahway was assigned Linden as his mission church, where he served until his transfer in 1926.

During these days of new beginnings, the Polish Roman Catholic people of Saint Theresa of the Little Flower of Jesus used the Greek church for services while their church was being built. In 1952, by order of Bishop Ivancho, Saint George's Church was elevated from its mission status to that of an established parish. The first permanent pastor was Reverend Father Michael J. Miyo. In 1958,

CHURCH EXTENSION,
St. Elizabeth Chapel, Linden, N. J
Franciscan Fathers.

INTERIOR OF SAINT ELIZABETH'S CHAPEL. This was the original site of the newly-formed church when it was located in a storefront. It was on West Blancke Street about where city hall is currently. (Courtesy L. Yeats.)

the church we see today was begun just over where the altar of the first church was. The cornerstone was set on July 3, 1960 with Monsignor George Billy as pastor.

Holy Trinity Polish National Catholic Church was organized in 1925. The Polish National Catholic Church secured the episcopate from the Old Catholic Church of Holland. Because the church received the episcopate from the Old Catholic source, the Polish National Catholic Church was the inheritor of Old Catholicism and the only Old Catholic body in the United States that was recognized by the See of Utrecht. Holy Trinity Church is located at 403 Ziegler Avenue.

The establishment of Saint Theresa of the Little Flower of Jesus Roman Catholic Church made history, as it was the first church in the United States to be dedicated to Saint Theresa of the Child Jesus following her canonization in Rome in May, 1925. The location of the first Mass was at Progress Hall, later known as the Lithuanian Liberty Park Hall, on Mitchell Avenue, with 20 people in attendance celebrated by Father Edward Kozlowski in August 22, 1925. The parish of Saint George's Greek Catholic Church offered the use of its church for worship until 1927.

June 27, 1926 was the groundbreaking ceremony and on November 7, 1926, the cornerstone was laid for the new church school. On Palm Sunday, April 10, 1927, the first mass in the new church was celebrated. Father Kozlowski desired

99

to separate the school from the church building in 1954, when the ground was broken for the new church. The following year on November 5, 1955, they celebrated the first mass in the new building. Father Kozlowski died in 1959. Reverend Stanislaus Stachowiak came as the new pastor. He coincidentally had been present in Rome on the day of Saint Theresa's canonization. In 1971, he became Pastor Emeritus of St. Theresa's Church, residing in the parish rectory and assisting in priestly duties until his death on May 12, 1976. In 1971, Father Vincent Bukowski became the pastor and worked with curates Father Chester Miodowski and Father Fred Miller. In 1980, Reverend Canon Walter Gorski became pastor. On June 19, 1993, Reverend Eugene Koch returned to become the pastor. In 1998, Saint Theresa's parish received Pastor Reverend Monsignor Bronislaw Wielgus.

Holy Family Roman Catholic Church held its first mass on January 15, 1939 in the Grasselli Community House. Prior to that date, a group of Slovak-speaking families met in homes to recite the Rosary together. The church building was blessed on November 30, 1941. The dream of the people of Tremley became a reality when Father Komar was appointed Resident Administrator in October 1955. The church was incorporated on November 20, 1956. In 1958, the former Grasselli Community House was purchased by the congregation and remodeled for church uses and named Father Komar Hall.

In October 1945, 300 Roman Catholic families from the Winfield Park area petitioned Archbishop Thomas J. Walsh to send a priest to celebrate mass for

SAINT THERESA OF THE CHILD JESUS INTERIOR, 1960. This was the original interior of Saint Theresa of the Child Jesus Church, built in 1955. (Courtesy L. Yeats.)

them, and on October 25, the archbishop appointed Father Charles Buttner as administrator of the mission in Winfield. He also appointed Father James F. Looney, vice chancellor of the archdiocese, to assist Father Buttner. On November 11, 1945, the first mass was celebrated in Winfield Park in the community auditorium. A census of the parish was conducted by Father Thomas F. Mulvaney in 1948 and indicated that the number of families had increased to 1,506. This caused the number of Sunday masses at the Winfield Community Center to be increased from two to three and St. John the Apostle parish was established June 4, 1948.

The first pastor appointed to this parish was Monsignor Mulvaney, who assumed his charge on June 19, 1948. Ground was broken for the church and school building on Valley Road on November 24, 1948 and the first mass was said in the basement chapel on September 11, 1949. On September 11, 1950, the new parish school opened. On November 2, 1950, the sisters moved into a newly completed convent, and on March 19, 1952, the priests of the parish moved into the new rectory.

Mulvaney's dedication was recognized. Pope John XXIII gave him the title of Right Reverend Monsignor. Monsignor Mulvaney had celebrated his 45th anniversary of ordination to the priesthood on March 7, 1970. Because of illness, he retired at the end of April. Mulvaney passed away on October 2, 1970, just 12 days after his retirement and testimonial dinner were held at Mother Seton High School.

Reverend Edward G. Price succeeded Mulvaney. In 1980, Father Alfonse Arminio succeeded Monsignor Price. In 1982, Father Arminio established a school board to serve as an advisory council to the principal and pastor. This board continues to serve the parish today. In that same year, Sister Donna Marie O'Brien, O.P., was named principal. In 1988, Arminio, who had previously served as Chaplain in the U.S. Navy, resigned and re-enlisted in order to serve his country again as Navy Chaplain. Since December 1988, Monsignor Richard M. McGuinness has served as pastor.

Raritan Road Baptist Church had its modest beginning on September 23, 1951. Under the leadership of George Bogan, at that time a student at Shelton College, services were held at the Community Center, Pallant Avenue and Raritan Road. After Bogan's ordination, he continued serving the church as first pastor. In 1957, the membership voted to purchase land located at Raritan Road and Coleman Avenue as a site for future church buildings. The present one-story chapel on this site was dedicated on February 1, 1958. Anticipating enlargement of the chapel, additional ground has been purchased.

In 1933, the Mount Moriah Baptist Church was organized in a small storefront on South Wood Avenue by Reverend A.R. Ross. The congregation worshipped there for two years. In 1935, the present church building was erected on land once owned by the Standard Oil Company.

On June 12, 1971, the interior of the church was destroyed by fire. Services were held for a short time at Reverend Bullock's church on 18th Street and later, at the senior citizen building on Dill Avenue. In 1973, the name of the church changed to the Greater Mount Moriah Baptist Church.

In May 1928, a small group of families, primarily of German descent, felt the need for a Lutheran church in Linden. The name St. Paul's Evangelical Lutheran Church was chosen at a meeting in the Polish National Church, and in September 1928 regular services in German and English were begun in the Craftsmen's Club in Linden with Herman Mackensen as acting superintendent. For ten years freight trains rumbling by on the tracks behind the building frequently interrupted Sunday services. The first permanent home for the congregation was purchased in February 1929 on the corner of East Elm Street and Moore Place. The Depression delayed construction of the new building, but the title was finally received on December 11, 1933. The church grew throughout the 1940s and a new parish house was dedicated October 2, 1955.

La Iglesia Cristiana de Linden (Christian Church of Linden) is also located at 45 East Elm Street at St. Paul's Lutheran Church. It was founded on October 3, 1996 by Pastor Roberto Montes de Oca.

Greater Promise Baptist Church was founded in July 1975 as the Greater Promise Baptist Mission. The congregation's first home was at 1149 St. Georges Avenue, Roselle. They moved to 912 Cranford Avenue under the leadership of Reverend W.E. Bland, and deacons Elsie Redding and Riley Johnson. A few years later the church moved to its current location at 1241 Union Street under the leadership of Rev. J. Brown. The current pastor is Reverend Paul E. Young.

White Rock Baptist Church began in Elizabeth with families meeting to worship and pray at residences until 1964 when a building was purchased at 198 East St. Georges Avenue under the leadership of Reverend James Bullock. He was ill at the time and died in 1967. He had left it in the capable hands of Reverend Lucius Phillips. In 2001 the City of Linden purchased the church site. The building is now located at 1101 Chandler Avenue. Reverend Robert C. Morris is the current pastor.

The Apostolic Outreach Assembly was chartered and co-founded by District Elder Joseph Flemmings and his wife Pastor Bernice Flemmings in 1976. The congregation then rented a building at 1175 St. Georges Avenue in Roselle for the first few years. Three years later they moved across the street to 1172 East St. Georges Avenue in Linden. Pastor Joseph passed away on September 11, 1995. Over the years, Elder Curtis Flemmings, Elder Larry Flemmings, and his wife Elder Kathy Flemmings have also become assistant pastors in this active church. The City of Linden purchased the property in April 2001, and the congregation met at private residences until May 2002 when phase one of their new building at 1014 Dill Avenue was ready for occupation.

10. THE JEWISH COMMUNITY

By 1905, Linden was home to the second-largest Jewish community in Union County. At the time, Linden was separated into two distinct municipalities, a borough and a township. Both had few streets, an abundance of farmland, and property for sale at affordable prices.

Congregation Agudath Achim Anshe, the city's first shul to boast its own home, moved into a building at 604 Chandler Avenue at St. Georges Avenue as early as 1911. This first building served the congregation until it moved to 1224 East St. Georges Avenue. Residents of the area nurtured fond hopes for the Agudath Achim Anshe district with its opportunities for expansion and progress. Tinsmiths, blacksmiths, and businessmen from New York settled here, and many purchased their property from the Litvinoffs, a family that had settled in the community and chosen real estate as a profession. Some of the early settlers included Joseph Hirschman, grocer Barok Slavin, tinsmith Samuel Galowitz, and tailor Samuel Platus. With St. Georges Avenue as the main street of this new metropolis, the congregation thrived until Jews began moving to the more suburban parts of the city.

Ahavas Achim Anshe of Tremley was another early congregation. Its incorporation papers listed a total of 11 charter members, including Samuel Mopsick (the founding president), Isadore Kalish, Joseph Samuel Duchin, Herman Coplan, Isaac Itzkowitz, Julius Levine, Morris Fishkin, Nathan Gimpeloff, and Solomon Duchin. Members held services at private homes until 1920, when the property between Wood Avenue and Clinton Street was donated by John Fedor as the site of a synagogue (often referred to as the Eighteenth Street Synagogue). Rabbi Louis Tabachnik was the first spiritual leader of Ahavas Achim Anshe, and after 33 years in the pulpit, he was succeeded by Rabbi Zachariash (1952–1954), followed by Rabbi Isaac Flam. In the late 1920s, the Ladies Auxiliary presented the congregation with two Torahs, and the happy occasion was celebrated with a parade through Linden in the traditional manner of their ancestors. The happy paraders were greeted by folks of all denominations along the parade route, and onlookers tossed coins into a Star of David flag as donations to the synagogue. There was also a band of New York musicians. Upon reaching the synagogue, the festivities continued with dancing and singing.

In 1914, a small group of immigrants from Eastern Europe rented space in the home of Samuel and Rebecca Berzon at 300 E. Price Street in order to conduct services and have a Hebrew school. This was the beginning of Congregation Anshe Chesed. During this early period, the members of the congregation attended High Holiday services at several locations in the eastern end of Linden where there was a larger Jewish population, including 1123 Hussa Street located east of the Baltimore & Ohio Railroad. This building later housed the United Paint and Varnish Company owned by Sid Mandel, who at one time was a cantor for the congregation. Services were conducted both by laymen and by a teacher named Elijah Solomon, who taught children from his home. Some of the early members of the congregation were the families of Harry Rabkin, Hyman Levine, Louis Kurland, Max Feinberg, Joseph Weitzman, Louis Feldstein, Barnet Rakin, David Winetsky, and Samuel Freiman. They were later joined by the families of Philip Weitzman, Jacob Siegel, Philip Margulies, Louis Levine, Joseph Engel, William Schmidt, and Adolph Braun.

In 1918, the congregation acquired property on East Blancke Street between Maple Avenue and Roselle Street, and constructed its first synagogue building, which still serves as a two-family home at 537 East Blancke Street.

By 1921, in the aftermath of World War I, the Jewish population in the area had increased and there was a need for a larger structure to serve as the synagogue. Land was purchased at the corner of East Blancke Street and Maple Avenue. In 1922, the building later known as the Blancke Street Synagogue opened and served the congregation for more than 30 years. The building at the corner of Maple and Blancke still functions today as the home of the Linden PAL.

A full-time rabbi, cantor, and teacher was provided when Rabbi Morris Baicofsky was engaged in 1921. He had just arrived from Bialystok, Poland, and his inspiration and store of religious knowledge gave the congregation a spiritual impetus that helped it grow beyond the dreams of its founders. Rabbi Baicofsky served until 1946 and remained as cantor until 1972. Finally, both the synagogue and the People's Lyceum (at 520 Elizabeth Avenue) were completed. The People's Lyceum, however, failed to receive financial support and was soon sold.

During the Great Depression Congregation Anshe Chesed Hebrew school was expanded to include a Sunday school, and the building enlarged to include two separate classrooms.

During World War II, Congregation Anshe Chesed played an important part in the world's Jewish scene. United Jewish Appeal, the Joint Distribution Committee, Zionist movements, and Yeshiva institutions all found willing workers and facilities at Congregation Anshe Chesed. The social area of the Anshe Chesed building was doubled in size, and extra seats were provided in the women's section of the sanctuary. In 1946, the congregation hired Rabbi Horowitz. He was succeeded by Rabbi Joseph Renov, whose tenure from 1947 to 1953 was marked by a period of transition and decision-making.

By 1952, the "Blancke Street Synagogue" was in need of extensive repairs and could not accommodate the congregation's growing membership. In addition, since the center of the Jewish population had shifted to the north side of St. Georges Avenue, the synagogue was no longer centrally located. In 1953, Rabbi Aharon Shapiro took up the active religious leadership and provided an intelligent and modern approach to traditional Judaism. Rabbi Yaacov Peterseil followed.

In May 1954, the northeast corner of St. Georges Avenue and Orchard Terrace was purchased for the location of a new synagogue and center. After two fund drives and many meetings, the congregation moved into the first section of its new building, now known as the school and activities section, prior to Rosh Hashanah in 1956. A third fund-raising drive helped to fund the construction of the sanctuary section of the building.

By 1951, a desire for conservatism crystallized in the minds of several younger members of Anshe Chesed. With Samuel Moritz as its principal spokesman, the group began to hold parlor meetings devoted to exploring the proposition of organizing a new congregation. The movement grew so rapidly that they held their own High Holiday services that year in the recreation room of the Anshe Chesed synagogue.

AHAVAS ACHIM ANSHE OF TREMLEY LADIES AUXILIARY. The congregation was presented with two Torahs and the happy occasion was celebrated with a parade through Linden to the 18th Street synagogue where the Torahs are seen held by two men in the center. The boat-like object at the left is a flag, heavy with coins tossed into it along the route of march. (Joseph Gale's Eastern Union, the Development of a Jewish Community.*)*

BLANCKE STREET SYNAGOGUE. By 1952, the synagogue was getting older. It then became home to the Linden Police Athletic League. This scene shows the interior of the synagogue as it was being transformed to hold a gymnasium for the PAL. (Courtesy Maureen Edwards.)

In November 1952, the nucleus of the new congregation purchased land at Kent Place and Deerfield Terrace and incorporated as the Suburban Jewish Center, with a membership of 70 people. Between that time and February 1954, when members began to use a small section of the center, religious services, Hebrew and Sunday school classes, and meetings were held in the various homes of members, in the Linden Public Library, in the Myles J. McManus Elementary School, and even in a tent pitched on vacant land. One year, a circus tent was suspended over the vacant portion of the land, and services were held there. The new building was dedicated in January 1957. The Hebraic name Temple Mekor Chayim was chosen by the membership because it aptly connoted its English equivalent, "fountain of life." In 2000, the congregation merged with that of the neighboring city of Cranford. The building became a senior center.

There were many notable figures in Linden's Jewish community and many who made significant contributions towards the development of the city. In the early 1900s, Joseph Weitzman rented a house on Roselle Street and commuted to Newark. Eventually, he entered the construction field and transferred his operations to Linden. Using timber, fieldstones, and other materials from the local area, Weitzman built the home of former township attorney Harold DePew, as well as the city's first motion picture theater, which was designed by architect Abraham J. Silverstein in 1927. Located at St. Georges and Chandler Avenues, the theater was the scene of many city meetings, as it was large enough to hold the crowds. Weitzman became a founder of Congregation Anshe Chesed and served as president longer than any man up to that time. Joseph Weitzman's son Harry was appointed to the Linden police force in 1919 and served for many years as the town's sole Jewish officer. He retired after 43 years on the job.

David Winetsky, kin to former township attorney Lewis Winetsky, opened one of the area's earliest tailor shops, and Nathan Kaplan, who came from New York, was famous as the town's first motorized peddler. Many stories have been told of Kaplan's sedan full of merchandise and his frantic struggle to raise its reluctant roof whenever rain ruined his curbside sales.

As more and more families arrived, Jews became influential in the city's industrial development and were responsible for many historic firsts. Adolph Braun became the first Jewish justice of the peace, presiding over a small-cause court located, for a time, in his own home. Seeking a road through Linden while driving from New Brunswick to New York, Braun came upon an Elm Street property and was enchanted with it. He soon bought the farm at 226 East Elm Street. Braun later owned a one-story factory where bathing suits were manufactured. Benjamin Slavin was one of the constables Braun used for the execution of warrants and the serving of summonses.

Samuel Mopsick, a New York tailor, came to Linden in 1904 and purchased a lot for $175 in the beautiful "countryside." Mopsick and Samuel Duchin began to sell real estate in the South Wood Avenue area, and Mopsick is considered the guiding light in the development of that neighborhood. Today, a street named Mopsick recalls the pioneer and the man.

Other early residents included the Rakin and Ladenson families, who owned grocery stores on Elizabeth Avenue in 1913 and on Roselle Street c. 1915. Max Kuznitz came from Elizabeth in 1923 and farmed at Tremley Point. Still another resident was Isaac Mehrman, who succumbed to the blandishments of Max and Philip Litvinoff, agents of the Realty Trust Company, in 1907. Many newcomers did business with the Realty Trust Company, and Mehrman, a builder, began construction of a store (with apartments above) on Elizabeth Avenue, across the street from where the People's Lyceum was to stand. The unfinished structure, however, was improperly braced and crumbled under the assault of a violent storm. Undaunted, Mehrman salvaged what he could and rebuilt the store and one apartment. It was a decade before his resources were sufficiently replenished to resume construction on a large scale. Today, many private homes near Washington Avenue and Henry and Elm Streets were built by Mehrman.

Between 1920 and 1938, Dr. Abraham Barr served the community as a physician; he was the first Jewish doctor to practice in Linden. In 1924, Joseph Engel, a contractor, built the first apartment house, at 18–20 East Price Street. In 1925, Louis Levine had the distinction of becoming the first Jewish member of the Linden Board of Education, a position he held for eight years. Other Jewish men rose to prominence in civic and political affairs. Philip Cohen was city attorney from 1929 to 1933, and Louis Rakin was was the city's first Jewish magistrate. Harry Mopsick was the Democratic (later an Independent) nominee to Congress from Union County. Rakin and city attorney Lewis Winetsky (who has held the position for 21 years) were mainly responsible for the formation of an organized Democratic party in Linden. Linden also produced such leaders as Emanuel Bedrick, superintendent of schools; Abraham J. Frankel, director of public welfare; and Jerome Krueger, councilman.

EARLY PAL BUILDING. *The building was at the corner of East Blancke and Maple Avenues. It was purchased from Congregation Anshe Chesed and was commonly known as the Blancke Street Synagogue. (Courtesy Edwards.)*

11. FIGHTING FOR FREEDOM

On October 28, 1764, an ox was roasted in front of Barnaby Shute's tavern, the Marquis of Granby, between the courthouse and the river, in a celebration marking the 100th anniversary of the purchase of Elizabeth Town from the Indians. But the celebration was dampened by word that Parliament was going to levy a stamp tax on the colonies on the first of November 1765. The Stamp Act, which imposed an internal tax on the people of the colonies; and customs taxes, are considered by many to be the primary causes of the Revolution. When the first cannonball of the Revolutionary War was fired in Massachusetts in 1775, the lives of all the men living in what is now Linden were affected. During the war (1775–1783), 18 battles and engagements took place on land that is today part of Union County. The dates and locations of these hostilities are as follows:

> Ash Swamp: May 1777 and June 1779
> Connecticut Farms (Union): June 7 and June 23, 1780
> Elizabethtown: December 17, 1776; January 25–30, 1780; and June 6, 1780
> Elizabethtown Point: July 21, 1778 and June 8, 1780
> Rahway Creek: September 30, 1777
> Rahway Meadows: June 26, 1781
> Springfield: December 17, 1776; February 1777; October 1779; and
>   June 23, 1780
> Spanktown (Rahway): 1777
> Westfield: March 8, 1777, and June 1777

Early in the Revolution the British navy, for which the American privateer fleet was no match, captured nearby Staten Island and made it one of its principal bases. Soon, the island became a Tory stronghold. The British quartered a large garrison of soldiers there and maintained control of the island for most of the war.

Across the water the area of Linden, while still part of Elizabeth Town, was a productive farming district, quiet and unprotected. It was an ideal spot for raids, and the British took full advantage of the situation. Periodically, either the British or the Tories would steal across the sound at night to Tremley Point Road to drive off cattle and steal supplies. In the winter of 1779, when the water was frozen over, the British found it particularly easy to raid Linden, as they could simply march across the ice. Hatfield wrote the following in his *History of Elizabeth*:

> It proved to be one of the severest winters on record. The cold set in early, and storm succeeded storm, piling up snow in every direction, until Jan. 3, 1780. The snow covered the earth to the depth from four to six feet, the roads were everywhere obstructed, and almost nothing could be had for the sustenance of the troops. The winter of 1779-80 was one of the most severe on record in this area. The Staten Island-Sound froze so deep it accommodated several hundred sleighs, 2,500 men and all their ammunition and baggage in an American raid on Staten Island from Elizabeth Town.

The circumstances of a few such raids were preserved in old letters and recounted in the *Linden Observer* on Thursday, October 17, 1940:

> Once the British took a pet heifer belonging to pretty Mary Alston Marsh, daughter of Moses Marsh, one of Linden's first settlers. She made up her mind to save the pet, so she contrived to stampede all the cattle the British were driving. The cattle fled in all directions, trampling a few redcoats and scattering, so that the British were forced to go back to Staten Island empty-handed. Mary went home safely with her pet heifer.

Most raids were staged during the dark of night. The following account appeared in *Rivington's Gazette*, a newspaper published at that time:

> On the night of the following Thursday, December 14, 1780 a party of royal horse-thieves, under the command of the celebrated Lewis Robbins made an incursion into Rahway. They set out for Westfield to seize Sheriff Marsh, but as the roads were bad, and probably learning that the sheriff was not at home, they turned back, and made their way to old David Miller's, capturing him, some of his sons, and his horses. Having paroled the old man because of his infirmities, they proceeded to Peter Trembly's, where they seized and robbed of all his money and papers. They took also a Peter Horn . . . but at the sudden discharge of a gun they paroled their prisoners and fled.

But the colonists did not stand idly by as their homes and property were damaged or stolen. In an anniversary issue, a *Linden Observer* article notes:

> One night the British were almost attacked by the colonials. In 1776, General Mercer and his men marched from Perth Amboy to Linden and camped near Peach Orchard Brook. Mercer assembled a secret fleet of

boats and barges for an invasion of Staten Island. His men were drilled for a surprise attack and everything pointed to a successful venture, but the night of the projected raid fate intervened. A storm arose and lashed the boats about, scattering them so that the colonials could not dream of crossing the sound. General Mercer marched back to Perth Amboy.

By November 30, 1776, General Howe and the British occupied Elizabeth Town. Amnesty was offered to those who took the oath of allegiance to the king, and many professed patriots became Tories. Within a few days, Hessian reinforcements arrived from Perth Amboy. Philip Waldeck's *Diary of the American Revolution* offers an insight into the nature of the area. Waldeck, the chaplain of the Third Waldeck Regiment of Hessian troops, penned the following:

> December 8–1776
> We left Amboy . . . to march 16 miles to Elizabeth Town, but because of the shortage of horses, the cannon could not be moved rapidly and we had to leave our baggage behind. Night came on and we were obliged to camp under free Heaven. We had to be on guard as we received word that four hundred rebels [American troops] were near us. At break of day, we continued our march: The road from Amboy to Elizabeth Town is unusually pleasant and level. To right and left one sees either cleared woods or beautiful orchards. Altogether, it seems to me that Jersey is more fertile, productive, and richly cultivated than any other Province through which we have passed. At one o'clock we arrived in Elizabeth Town where we met the Hessian Regiment.

It also seems that the pesky and ever-present mosquito caused some difficulties during the war. Writing in his diary during July 1778, Waldeck reported:

> The hands and faces of our troops are quite swollen from mosquitoes. The heat is almost unbearable, the nights hotter than is the hottest daytime in our own country. Never have the mosquitoes been as troublesome as in these terribly hot days. The inhabitants light fires near the four sides of their houses; the smoke is intended to keep the insects out of their bedrooms, but it helps very little; their number does not diminish although the odor of smoking old rags, shoes, and other evil smelling things is in the air. In our tents they are in even greater numbers. . . .

> Today I saw a cow running, surely she had as many mosquitoes on her as she had hairs in spots, they sat in bunches like bees when ready to hive; just as many again swarmed about the poor beast; as they could not alight, they accompanied her. The cow ran into the water and then the swarms flew above her, as though waiting for her to come out. . . .

> When [the mosquitoes] are hungry they are so light in weight, that the wind blows them like a grain of barley. For mosquito invasions of dust, but after they have sat here in Staten Island as long ago as a minute they have sucked so much blood from our men.

As a side note to the mosquito situation, in 1901 Dr. John B. Smith of Rutgers University persuaded the New Jersey state government to appropriate $10,000 to drain salt marshes, and Elizabeth cooperated in his campaign, though he found other cities not so helpful. Although Dr. Smith failed to achieve a major victory, he is credited with having laid the groundwork for modern mosquito control.

By February 1779, the British were anxious to capture Governor William Livingston, the first governor of New Jersey after the signing of the Declaration of Independence, who was living in Elizabeth Town, and several unsuccessful attempts were made. Finally, a bribe of several thousand guineas was offered by Cortland Skinner as payment for the assassination of Livingston. The man to whom the money was offered was one Ephraim Marsh Jr., very likely a resident of the section later known as Linden, but he rejected the offer and Governor Livingston continued to be a thorn in the side of the British.

The year 1781 was marked by renewed partisan war. The loyalists seemed bent on visiting as much vengeance as possible on their rebel neighbors. Again, two newspaper extracts place the scenes in what is now Linden. These incidents were documented in Clayton's *History of Union and Middlesex Counties* as having appeared in the *New York Gazette* and the *Weekly Mercury* on February 7, 1780. Other reports of the skirmishes in the area can be found in *Documents Relating to the Colonial History of the State of New Jersey* held by the New Jersey Archives.

> On [Saturday] the 21st, a Party of about seventy of the enemy came over to Elizabeth Town from Staten Island. They landed at Halstead's Point, and were discovered between that place and the town by Capt. Hendricks who was patrolling with about ten or twelve men, and though so much inferior in number he kept a smart fire on them, which prevented them from penetrating farther into town than Doctor Winans. After collecting a few horses, etc. firing through the windows in the room where Mrs. Winans was, by which a boy was wounded in the arm, and burning the house of Mr. Ephraim Marsh they went off to their boats.

> Last night a detachment of the garrison of about thirty-six men, including two sergeants, under the command of Lieutenants Hutchinson and Barton, First Battalion New Jersey Volunteers with about thirty-four refugees and militia, under the command of Captains Durham and Robert landed at Trembly's Point, near the mouth of Rahway River, and surrounded the Tavern, in order to take three rebel

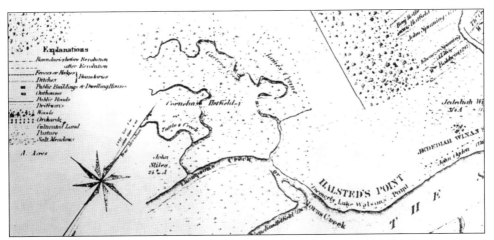

MAP OF TREMLEY AREA. *This map shows the area at the time of the Revolution. It was drawn by Ernest L. Myer. (Courtesy UCHS.)*

light horse, whose business was to patrol down the Sound and to give notice of any troops coming from Staten Island, but unfortunately those fellows were gone to Westfield. The troops then proceeded to one Capt. Amos Morse who was surprised and taken out of bed with four other rebels; after this they took between thirty and forty head of cattle, amongst which are six good oxen and about eighty sheep, which were drove to Trembly Point. The rebels collected to the amount of about forty, harassing the rear as usual. Lieutenant Hutchinson formed an ambush unperceived by the rebels, which had its desired effect. Fifteen rebels passed, hallooing, "Damn the refugees Cut then down!" Up the troops arose from the place where they were secreted. The rebels observing this, stood aghast, threw down their arms, others stood with arms in their hand. On this occassion ten were made prisoners.

Some time after this about twenty rebels collected near Trembly Point, on whom a charge was made and some taken prisoners, the troops and the refugees then embarked with the greatest regularity and good order, with all their cattle and sheep and came safe to Staten Island; not one of the troops received the least injury; one of the refugees received a spent ball on his thigh, which had no other effect than leaving its mark. The troops and refugees behaved with the greatest bravery on this occasion; twenty rebels are made prisoners, two of whom are wounded; some were killed, its not doubted, but several were wounded, as several were heard to scream and holler. The names of the prisoners follows- Capt. Amos Morse, Isaac Marsh, Z. Everet, Hambleton Roberts, George Mitchel Deeds, Isa Haynes, William Brant, Richard Lee, Jacob Brookfield, Gershon Brookfield, Jeremiah Bird, Isaac Drake, Ashe

Coddington, David Thorp, John Tucker, David Hetfield, Joseph Hynes, William Oliver, Sr., Ebenezer Williams and William Oliver.

After the surrender of General Charles Cornwallis in October 1781, skirmishes between the Staten Island forces and the "rebel Jersey inhabitants" continued, but these were only sporadic ruptures accompanying the last of the long conflict. A provisional treaty was signed in November 1782, and hostilities were ended in the spring of 1783. The eight-year struggle for independence was over.

The War of 1812 had at least one Linden casualty. In Rahway in 1912, to commemorate the war, a tribute was held in Rahway Cemetery to honor those who fell during this event. Private John Noe, one of those mentioned, was from the Linden area.

The American Civil War began on April 12, 1861, when Confederate general P.G.T. Beauregard opened fire on Fort Sumter in Charleston Harbor, South Carolina, and lasted until May 26, 1865, when the last Confederate army surrendered. The township of Linden became a new municipality just before the start of the war, on March 4, 1861.

Author and historian Jean-Rae Turner of the Union County Historical Society discusses some of the difficulties Linden and other area soldiers faced at the start of the Civil War:

VETERANS NAVAL PARADE ON BROAD STREET, 1893. This image is from a stereoview card. Our Linden men participated in this parade in Elizabethtown. (Courtesy L. Yeats.)

Many of the raw recruits who enlisted in the volunteer regiments responding at the "first call to arms" were not acquainted with using Springfield rifles. Unlike their grandfathers or great-grandfathers who had left to defend their farms during the Revolutionary War with their shotguns, the local recruits in the Civil War were inexperienced in hunting small or large game.

David Hatfield of Elizabethtown, who was elected captain in Company A, First Regiment, had some experience in the Mexican War. But the defeat and stampede at the first Battle of Bull Run, showed how woefully unprepared he and his fellow enlistees truly were. Meanwhile, calls went out for more and more men. Companies that formed in the Elizabeth area included Companies G and K of the Ninth Regiment, which was dubbed "The Jersey Blues," a name that had been made popular during the Revolutionary War.

As the war continued, officers were sent home to assist with recruitment. Captain William R. Meeker of Elizabeth and Lieutenant John B. Lutz of Company K, Third Regiment, who had been wounded, taken prisoner, and released, stood in front of a recruitment meeting in Elizabeth and urged the men to enlist. (Company K was the only volunteer outfit to be designated a "flying battery." They were then renamed the Sixth New York Cavalry Battery against their wishes to remain as Company K. History books list their victories as New York victories.) Still, the demand for more men continued. Unlike the South, the Union failed to place new recruits into old regiments. Instead, new, inexperienced regiments were formed. Eventually, many of the original companies were disbanded and the remaining men sent home. Some re-enlisted. Some did not. Jean-Rae Turner states, "In their efforts to recruit, the counties began to offer bounties. Essex County paid more than Union County, so Union County residents went there to enlist. Many of the bounty recipients collected, deserted and re-enlisted elsewhere to collect another bounty and desert again."

The recruiters even traveled to Europe for men when volunteerism failed. One of the recruits in Germany was Joseph Pulitzer, whose name is associated with the journalism prizes. But on March 3, 1863, the United States Congress approved the draft. Although there were reports of riots in Newark, the people in Elizabeth and Linden appeared to accept the draft without incident, but the draft itself was unsuccessful. It had too many loopholes. A person who did not wish to serve could pay a substitute soldier $300 to serve, and there were many exemptions. In all, New Jersey supplied 40 regiments and exceeded its quota of 79,348 by 10,057 men.

Three years after the Civil War ended, on May 5, 1868, the head of an organization of former Union soldiers and sailors—the Grand Army of the Republic—established Decoration Day. Major General John A. Logan declared it should be May 30, and the first large observance was held that same year at Arlington National Cemetery. On May 30, 1911, at the Veterans Cemetery at Rosehill Cemetery in Linden, a memorial service was held and remarks were

RE-DEDICATION OF WHEELER PARK. People gathered after improvements were made by the Union County Park Commission. From left to right are Charles Crane, Lois Lindlar (Wheeler's niece), Freeholder Nicholas Scutari, Joan Drake (Wheeler's niece), Mayor John T. Gregorio, and Council President Robert Bunk. (Courtesy Joan Drake.)

given by Frank Bergen at the dedication of a plot for graves of veterans of the Grand Army. In 1966, Congress and President Lyndon Johnson declared Waterloo, New York, the "birthplace" of Memorial Day, and the Army and Navy adopted regulations for proper observance at their facilities. After World War I, the day was expanded to honor those who have died in all American wars, and in 1971, Memorial Day was declared a national holiday by an act of Congress and was placed on the last Monday in May.

World War I, which lasted from 1914 until 1918, personally affected the residents of Linden, and a monument located in Woodrow Wilson Park honors the city's fallen heroes of that conflict: John Dobosievwicz, Joseph Urbanowitz, Samuel Weinberg, George Walsko, Oscar Kaplan, John Russell Wheeler, Walter Perkins, and Boleslaw Zygmunt.

In 1918 a U.S. Marine, John Russell Wheeler, died at the age of 23 in the battle of Belleau Wood, France, making him the first Union County resident to be killed in World War I. Born in Kearny, Wheeler moved to Linden when he was just nine years old; he attended School No. 1 and graduated from the twelfth grade along with two girls in his entire graduating class. In 1920, John Russell Wheeler Park was thus named in his honor, and when the Veterans of Foreign Wars Post #1397 in Linden received its charter on September 27, 1925, it was named the John Russell Wheeler Post by its 12 founding members: Charles H. Tangerman, Dominic A. Valvano, Martin Palamar, Eric W. Murphy, Joseph V. Casino, Michael

JOHN C. AND ELECTA V. WHEELER. The couple is shown here celebrating their 50th wedding anniversary. From 1905, they lived at 306 South Stiles Street. They were the parents of H. Roy Wheeler, mayor of Linden, and John Russell Wheeler, who was the first Linden man killed in action during World War I. (Courtesy Joan Drake.)

JOHN RUSSELL WHEELER. Wheeler was the first Linden man killed in action during World War I. John Russell Wheeler Park of the Union County Park Service and the Linden Post VFW are named for him. (Courtesy Joan Drake.)

117

J. Connelly, Meyer Gerson, Frank Wiskosky, Irving B. Fowler, Robert Golden, Joseph Angelo, and John M. Caruso.

In 1919, President Woodrow Wilson named November 11 Armistice Day in honor of the truce that had ended World War I a year earlier, and on that day, in 1925, two commemorative tablets were unveiled at School No. 1 in Linden to honor those who enlisted as soldiers in World War I. The borough tablet, located on the corner of Curtis Street, lists the following names:

George Ashworth
Austin Baldwin
Clifford Baldwin
Charles Beetle
Robert Beetle
Spurgeon Beetle Jr.
C. Dudley Blancke
Herbert Bundy
Roy Bundy
Joseph Casino
Robert Eaton
William Gourley
Henry Hardenburg Jr.

William Hartman
Anthony Koch
Joseph Koch
Matthew Koch
Daniel Kluge
William Kluge
John Lambert
Harold MacDowell
Stephen Mannuzza
Vincent Mannuzza
Leo McDonagh
George Miller
Ernest Miller

LINDEN HOME GUARD. The Home Guard are pictured here at ceremonies on the front lawn of School No. 1 before the parade on July 4, 1918. The war would end five months later. (Courtesy Edward Hering.)

Edward Mitchell Jr.
John Monsoon Jr.
Andrew More Jr.
Leonard A. More
Joseph Modrak
Henry Opple
George Paye

Lloyd Roll
Sigmund Schafanovich
Dominic Valvano
Frank Villani
Harry Wagner
Harry Weitzman

Located on the corner of Gibbons Street, the township tablet is inscribed as follows: "This tablet is erected by the township of Linden in honor of its one hundred seventy nine men who served in the World War and in perpetual remembrance of their number who lost their lives in the service." The soldiers listed on the tablet are:

Joseph Angelo
Frank Barr
William Berlinski
John Byko
Percy Carkuff
Anthony Cook
Edward Dillon
Martin Derrig
John Dobosiewicz
Seare Dougherty
John Feehan
Ida Feinberg
Samuel Feinberg
Joseph Gabrick
Joseph Gaydos
Elmer Gibbs
Nathan Gushin
Fred Haefner
Romain Harris
Andrew Hicky
Harry Hickman
Roy Hickman
Michael Hudak
William Hurst
Charles Jacob
John Jacobi
Alexander Jagodinski
Oscar Kaplan
James Kenworthy
Henry Klubenspies

William Kraemer
William Krasnowski
George Leyerle
Fred Lichti
Thomas Lichti
William Lindsay
Theodore Lodge
Joseph Loitch
Ernest Mahar
John Mahar
Philip Marshefsky
Garrett Maye
James Maye
Sam Mehrman
John Miller
Leonard Moore
Peter Murin
William Niemeck
Edward Nusse
John Oriechowski
Edward Pellinger
Walter Perkins
Walter Pfitzenmayer
Elmer Pierce
Henry Potter
Ferdinand Rechinitzer
Walter H. Roll
Marion Romanowski
James Runyon
Edward Sanford

William Semlar	Albert Weber
Charles Smith	Hugo Wendel
Richard Smith	John Russell Wheeler
Rolland Smith	Albert Wilke
John Steffen	John Willick
Joseph Urbanowitz	Bernard Wosniak
Robert Walker	Charles Wosniak
George Walsko	Charles Zbranek
Bert Walters	Boleslaw Zygmant

A local military unit, the Linden Home Guard, was also available for service on the homefront. After working their regular jobs, members of this unit drilled and held themselves at readiness, but, despite being outfitted in uniforms and supplied with military equipment, which were obtained through voluntary contributions, the home guards did not hold any official authority until they were reorganized on December 28, 1917 as the New Jersey State Militia Reserves. The group was officially activated on February 27, 1918, and Jules Verner became the leader of Linden's local group. Clarence H. Smith was first lieutenant and Thomas A. Archipley, second lieutenant. The non-commissioned officers included A.H. Gibson, John Potter, W. Hinoholiffe, Peter Lindsay, Vincent Keil, H. Pedersen, Norman Anderson, and J.I. Bowblis, and the entire enrollment was 132 men.

Among the memorable duties performed by these reservists was standing guard in Perth Amboy—following a devastating explosion in Morgan—to prevent the looting of evacuated homes in the case of a similar disaster. The militia reserves also held sentry at the Standard Oil Works in Linden. At the Aircraft Works, the men performed guard duty at the request of the company following a "bomb scare." The bomb threat turned out to be a false alarm.

World War I also saw the establishment in Linden of many volunteer organizations whose members knitted socks and made bandages, among other tasks. One group, the Linden Soldiers Aid Society, organized on October 17, 1917, aimed "to keep the boys in smokes." After functioning successfully for the duration of the war, they disbanded shortly after the termination of hostilities.

A World War I aircraft manufacturer, the Standard Aircraft Corporation—which originated on Long Island—was the first to arrive in the Linden area, relocating there in 1918. In that year, the Handley-Page 0-400 heavy bomber, with a 100-foot wingspan, was built by the company, and complete sets of parts for at least 100 such planes were shipped to England that summer. At its height, Standard Aircraft Corporation employed 1,000 people, but the firm went bankrupt and was sold at auction in 1919. According to David P. Winans, editor of the New Jersey Aeronautical Historical Society's newsletter The Skeeter, the Handley-Page bomber was the largest land plane in America during World War I. Interestingly, one of the bombers crashed along the Elizabeth River after taking off from the "Bayway Airfield," which was the property around the Standard Aircraft

JOSEPH OWENS SR. Owens served in World War II from 1941 to 1945 in New Hebrides, Okinawa, and Sipan. (Courtesy Joseph Owens.)

site, on March 10, 1919. The plane was en route to Philadelphia and was carrying a piano in its bomb bay as part of a test. The engines failed and the aircraft crash-landed. One person was reported hurt during this test.

World War II ended on September 2, 1945, with the formal surrender of Japan aboard the U.S. battleship *Missouri* in Tokyo Bay. Some 16.5 million Americans took part in this war; about 400,000 of them died in service, more than 290,000 of those in battle.

Linden welcomed home its veterans with a huge celebration on Saturday, April 6, 1946, that included a parade beginning at Russell Wheeler Park. The parade's colorbearers included Lieutenant Patricia McIntyre of the Army Nurse Corps; Frank Slugal Jr., a paratrooper in the 82nd Airborne Division; Paul A. Wieser, U.S. Navy and a member of the crew of the U.S.S. *North Carolina*; and Sergeant Daniel D. Dvorin, Air Force. The grand marshal of the day's festivities was Marine Charles Hemenway, who had been presented with the Navy Cross, the highest award of the United States Naval Service, for his unselfish bravery.

Another local World War II hero was Frank Gaboda. Born in a Lower Road farmhouse on February 19, 1923, Gaboda, along with his family, soon moved to a house on West Seventeenth Street across from an open parcel of land known as the Seventh Ward Park. On December 14, 1942, Gaboda enlisted in the U.S. Marine Corps, and on January 13, 1944, his unit moved into action in the Asiatic-Pacific Theater. He saw action in the fight for the Marshall Islands from January 31 to February 5, 1944, and when the Marines landed on Saipan Island in the Marianas Group on June 5, 1944, Gaboda was among them. On July 10, 1944, he covered his platoon's advance with his Browning automatic rifle, boldly moving ahead of the unit through terrain that afforded ideal cover to the enemy. Gaboda was personally responsible for killing at least 20 of the enemy before he was mortally wounded while leading his group across an exposed position. For this "aggressive determination and courageous fighting spirit," he was posthumously awarded the Silver Star and Purple Heart. Frank Gaboda's body is interred in the Punchbowl National Cemetery in Honolulu, Hawaii. He had three brothers—George, Emil, and John—who also served their country in this war. John died

Sergeant Edward Hering. Hering was armament crew chief of the 501st Bomb Group, 485 Bomb Squadron. N.W. Field Guam World War II 20th Airforce Veteran. (Courtesy Edward Hering.)

while in the Army, but George and Emil returned to Linden. Gaboda also had four sisters—Pauline Mesko, Helen Stanch, Mary Mays, and Dorothy Genievich—who still reside in the old family home.

Several honor rolls were erected throughout the city as memorials to Linden's 102 fallen heroes of World War II. These soldiers are as follows:

Basile, Vincent	Jensen, Arthur R.
Battaglia, John	Jonas, Edward
Beriont, Walter	Jordan, David
Best, Stanley J.	Kalish, Norbert
Biek, Cornelius G.	Kaplan, Seymour
Blackman, Abraham M.	Karpas, Peter J.
Boyer, Henry A.	Kelly, James W.
Brazilian, Milton W.	King, Ernest
Brosky, Robert J.	Knott, James Patrick
Capp, Peter Jr.	Komar, Michael
Carson, Walter R.	Kostick, Alexander W.
Cebula, Stanley J.	Krill, Michael
Chiravelle, John A.	Laci, Joseph
Chrobak, Michael M.	Lawson, Clifford M.
Dalcher, Harold T.	Lazo, George
Danowski, Martin M.	Lever, Robert T.
DeGaetano, Samuel	Levine, Sidney A.
Disbrow, Clifford H.	Likowski, Henry
Fagan, Francis Wesley	Littlehales, Roy W.
Fircha, John	McCarthy, John J.
Fonda, Fred A.	Maffia, Alfred P.
Frentz, Henry Jr.	Mehrman, Samuel
Furman, Charles W.	Martone, Ralph Jr.
Gaboda, Frank	Maul, Warren
Gaboda, John	Michaluk, Stanley
Gerhard, Walter J. Jr	Mihalko, Andrew
Goglozinski, Frank J.	Moyle, Chester W.
Grant, John S.	Mulhall, Edwin J.
Green, Russell W.	Myers, Milton W.
Grohmann, Richard C.	Newell, Frank
Guerra, Joseph	Nixon, William J.
Haefner, Richard W.	Palys, Stanley J.
Haines, William G. Jr.	Panno, Thomas
Harvan, Michael J.	Paserba, Walter
Henry, Kenneth F.	Pecherow, Morris
Hergenhan, Francis E.	Phillips, Joseph J.
Horowitz, Jacob	Pietrowski, Edward C.
Iaanarilli, Mario	Rader, Samuel I.

Rakin, Israel A.

Rizzo, Basil

Ropose, James G.

Sabak, Michael

Schroeder, Henry

Sczepaniak, William L.

Senise, Raymond Joseph

Shirlaw, John J.

Shupek, John

Silberstein, Seymour J.

Slahetka, Walter

Spevack, Harold

Spittler, Cecil

Stadnick, Robert

Tarasewicz, Joseph B.

Tobin, Paul G.

Wales, Alexander H.

Wardenski, John A.

Weitowic, Phillip

Wesolowski, Albert

Wighton, John

Wilke, Edward F.

Wishosky, Adolph

Wright, Columbus

Zwarum, Michael Jr.

Zavoda, Michael

A memorial plaque located at Congregation Anshe Chesed lists the following names of deceased soldiers from the disbanded Jewish War Veterans Linden Post No. 437, of which Mike Dupkin was commander: Robert Alberts, David Atkins, Abraham M. Blackman, Gerald R. Dopkin, Jacob Horowitz, Norbert Kolish, Seymour Kaplan, Sidney A. Levine, Morris Perchow, Herbert Monash, Samuel A. Rader, Seymour Silberstein, Israel A. Rakin, and Samuel Mehrman.

Of particular note is Samuel Mehrman, who perished in a mysterious accident at sea. The following article, an *Associated Press* news release that was saved by Perry Leib for a number of years, addressed the events of his strange disappearance:

> Washington, D.C., June 2 1948. What happened to a treasure-laden transport and occupants that disappeared off the Africa Gold Coast. The plane vanished Dec. 4, 1945, as completely as if it had evaporated. It was on a routine 700-mile flight carrying an undisclosed amount of gold and silver from its home field near Monrovia, Liberia to Accra, British West Africa. Within 12 hours a search was started by air and by sea and it eventually covered 112,500 square miles without turning up so much as a burned matchstick. Experts have decided that the pilot, Lieutenant Oliver K. Morton of Wichita, Kansas may have flown about 20 miles to sea to avoid a storm and the plane may have crashed without leaving any floating wreckage. The crew included Corp. Samuel Mehrman of Linden, New Jersey, Corp. Samuel K. Klink of Irvington, New Jersey and Sergeant Seymour J. Stanger of New York. Among the passengers was Second Lieutenant Walter H. Nelson, of White Plains, N. Y.

Research through the old *Linden Observer* newspapers through the World War II years shows that several Linden soldiers were held as prisoners of war. However, there were few details available or printed, except in one case. Corporal Paul Werkmeister, former 9th Ward Councilman and mayor of Linden, was serving with the 422nd Battalion of the 106th Infantry when his unit was cut off during the Battle of the Bulge in December, 1944. Werkmeister's unit was cut off by German troops. The Americans were then marched 140 miles to a camp at Muhlberg, about 80 miles south of Berlin. According to the *Linden Leader* of April 26, 1973, Werkmeister lost 40 pounds in 4 months and "was so weak, I couldn't make up my bed in the morning." There was a "miserable diet" of thin soup made with potatoes and turnips, although stockpiles of food were found when the Russians liberated the area on April 23, 1945. Werkmeister met another Linden man, William Melichar, in the German camp. On sighting Werkmeister, Melichar cracked, "This sure ain't Linden." Werkmeister had returned home on leave because he was a prisoner more than 90 days, a policy instituted by the Army. Werkmeister recalled those days in Germany, which may typify the experiences of soldiers anywhere: "You wonder, 'How did this happen to me?' You feel it's not happening to you. You wonder from day to day if you're going to live or die, and the feeling is indescribable when you're released. It's like being reborn."

Military authorities had recognized Linden as one of the three most strategic areas in the continental United States, and so the local defense council, organized on June 5, 1941, formulated and carried out a program of community protection that involved emergency defense training, air-raid precaution, emergency police and firefighters, a decontamination corps, and the creation of a unique intra-city communication system routed through a control center. Lindenites donated

PAUL WERKMEISTER. The former mayor served as an Army sergeant in World War II in the 106th Infantry, 422nd Regiment. This 1943 image is outside 141 Munsell Avenue. (Courtesy Paul Werkmeister.)

WILDCAT. The plane is inspected at Linden airport. Navy pilots would take them up for test flights before they were put onto aircraft carriers for combat in World War II. (Courtesy UCHS.)

blood in an effort coordinated by the defense council in cooperation with the American Red Cross. Through the office of the defense council, there were also drives for the collection of clothing, tin cans, and waste fats. Lindenites worked hard on the homefront, helping Linden's industries to provide such things as planes to cover the decks of fighting carriers, oil and grease to fuel the war machines, silk to make parachutes, machine tools to furnish replacements, and chemicals and gases to use in medical services.

One such important wartime industry was the L.J. Wing Manufacturing Company, located at 2300 North Stiles Street. During its day, Wing supply and exhaust fans were "on-the-job" in industrial plants throughout much of North America. Others ventilated the ships of the Merchant Marine, the U.S. Navy, and the Coast Guard. Wing fans with special construction features were installed at vital national defense sites. Numerous other products were built regularly by Wing to fill tomorrow's industrial needs and carried the name of Wing and of Linden far and wide. The company had maintained this aim: "that the products it makes shall be the finest in quality, performance and engineering concept."

The Eastern Aircraft Division of General Motors Corporation was the second airplane manufacturer to locate in Union County, and the Wildcat fighter rolled off the assembly line at the company's plant on Route 1 in Linden. When the General Motors plant had first opened in 1937, it was used for the assembly and testing of Buick, Oldsmobile, and Pontiac automobiles, but the outbreak of World War II ended the production of these pleasure cars and the lines were shut down. Plant management made efforts to obtain government contracts to continue operation. When all seemed hopeless, it was discovered that the U.S. Navy needed more facilities in which to produce the FM-1 Wildcat, designed by Grumman Aircraft Engineering Corporation of Bethpage, Long Island. With this knowledge, the General Motors Corporation formed the Eastern Aircraft Division, and its Linden plant became a part of that division on January 21, 1942. Representatives from the Linden plant were sent to Bethpage to learn how to make the carrier-based fighter planes. The automobile assembly lines were removed, and the roof of the building was raised 26 feet to make room for the planes. An addition was also built onto the rear of the building. New sources of raw materials and standard parts also had to be found because most of Grumman's suppliers were operating at full capacity.

Employees that had been assembling automobiles were retrained to assemble planes. Supervisory programs were conducted at the Grumman plants, while other trainees were sent to other aircraft firms to learn how airplane engines, propellers, and instruments were assembled and installed. The New Jersey State Training School, the Delehanty Institute, and area colleges such as New York University all offered courses between February and October 1942. Schools in Elizabeth gave two- to eight-week courses for more than 1,000 men and women.

In addition, the Navy wanted the assembly line in Linden to be interchangeable with Grumman's. As a result, the so-called PK ships were developed. The name came from the Parker-Kalon fasteners attached temporarily to all parts. A large

GENERAL MOTORS POSTCARD. The plant opened in 1937 and manufactured cars. During World War II General Motors formed the Eastern Aircraft division in Linden on January 21, 1942.

machine shop was built at Linden, and numerous subcontractors were found to make some of these parts. They worked with a group of Elizabeth and Hillside teachers in a former Newark jewelry factory on some of these parts as inspectors. As the men were called to war, the women were called on to build the planes. The Linden plant boasted many "Rosie the Riveters."

As the war continued, the company needed more room. The Eastern Aircraft Division negotiated with the Gordon's Gin plant nearby to use their warehousing facilities for its purchasing and accounting departments. The facility became part of the Eastern Aircraft Division on September 1, 1942.

Meanwhile, across Route 1, work was progressing on a new airport. An eight-plane hangar was constructed, and macadam runways were placed on the clay-based field. On August 31, 1942, the first Wildcat, which had been towed across the highway earlier, was successfully tested before several thousand employees. Production went into full gear. Even as the planes were being produced, changes were being made. Some of these were the result of battlefront experience. In one instance, the Navy demanded a change in the number of guns. That change alone required some 4,000 engineering orders. Early in 1943, the FM-2 began to replace the FM-1 on the assembly line. Soon, the Linden plant became the only plant in the nation making the FM-2, which was designed to fly from merchant ships that had been converted to small aircraft carriers. Both the FM-1 and FM-2 Wildcats were produced throughout 1943. The plant continued to improve its tooling, also, and production was at its peak in April 1944. The new airport usually had long lines of Wildcats waiting to be delivered to both the American and British Navy.

HANGARS OF LINDEN AIRPORT, 1994. The airport was razed and rebuilt farther back from Route 1 from 1997 to 1998. The area from Stiles Street now includes a major shopping area that is home to Target and other stores. A movie theater and a hotel are also planned for the site. (Courtesy UCHS.)

GORDON'S GIN. This business was located on Edgar Road and Route 25 on March 9, 1935. (Courtesy L. Yeats.)

Late in August 1944, the Navy began to decrease the number of Wildcat fighters it required. Soon production ceased. When the war ended, General Motors Corporation converted back to an automobile assembly line, with production resuming in 1946. Truck production began in 1992 and continues to the present day. The airfield was turned over to the city of Linden and became the homeport of the area Civil Air Patrol.

Another legacy of the World War II era, the Winfield Park Township was originally designed as a housing project for workers in the Kearny shipyards and other wartime workers in New Jersey. It was named the Winfield Park Mutual Housing Corporation at a meeting during its formation that was held at the Winfield Scott Hotel in Elizabeth. The hotel was named after Winfield Scott, a hero of Elizabeth from the War of 1812 and the Civil War.

The land that Winfield Park encompasses was once part of the Sperry Farm and includes a full 110 acres of former City of Linden and Clark Township property, as the farm was located in both municipalities. This community of 700 housing units began on a hectic note as the Federal Public Housing Authority was seeking locations for the project. Many communities in Union and other counties turned a deaf ear to appeals from housing authorities for permission to locate the project within their boundaries.

"CHRISTIE TANKS." They were manufactured in Linden at the Christie Tank Company for the United States Army, on St. Georges Avenue near Stiles Street. In the upper row at far right is J. Walter Christie. (Courtesy Edward Hering.)

The community was also the subject of a Senate investigation under the direction of then-senator Harry S. Truman, who headed a special committee investigating war contracts. This was followed by an FBI inquiry and glaring newspaper and magazine headlines. These inquiries dealt mostly with construction problems. Five months before the first tenants moved in, the state legislature overrode a veto of former governor Charles A. Edison and enacted into law the bill incorporating the new Township of Winfield. The township became immediately unique in that it was believed to be the only incorporated municipality. The sale of the property was finally consummated during the summer of 1941. The first tenants moved into Winfield Park on December 1, 1941, and James E. Thompson, one of the first residents, a shipyard worker, a prime mover in establishing the housing project, and the first president of the Winfield Park Mutual Housing Corporation, was named one of the three temporary members of the township committee, pending the first election. The other two named were Henry E. King, a trustee of the housing corporation, and John B. Fennelly, a resident.

Since that time, the township has been governed by a committee that consists of three members, one elected each year for a three-year term. Other offices such as a town clerk, treasurer, assessor, collector, municipal magistrate, police chief, and fire chief are also maintained. A board of education is also elected, with three members each year, each for completion of three-year terms. Union County's 21st municipality, Winfield Park Township has had a short but interesting life in the 61 years since its establishment.

The Korean War began on June 25,1950, when communist North Korea moved south across the 38th parallel to invade the Republic of Korea. The United States joined United Nations forces from 16 countries to defend South Korea by pushing the communists north. The Korean War was one of the hardest fought wars in United States history: 54,246 Americans died, including MIAs and those lost or buried at sea, and 103,284 were wounded. Linden lost six of its own sons during this conflict: Leo P. Russavage, Charles Gahm Jr., Richard A. Kanski, John V. Hemenway, George D. Libby, and Ronald F. Mc Govern. Finally, on July 27, 1953, a truce to end the conflict was signed, but troops still face one another today over a narrow demilitarized zone.

Veterans of the Korean War may recall their encounters with the formidable Russian-built T-34 tanks, which actually had their origins in Linden. J. Walter Christie, an inventor, set up a small factory off St. Georges Avenue near Stiles Street for the construction of a newly designed tank. In all, nine Christie tanks rolled off his assembly line during 1931. Seven of these went to the U.S. Army for testing, while the other two (along with a manufacturing license) were sold to Soviet Russia.

Older residents of Linden may recall seeing and hearing those 10-ton vehicles as they charged about the open fields of the city. While neither the U.S. Army nor the British Army did little beyond testing the extremely fast tanks, the Russians eventually evolved the design into their T-34, which they used in both World War II and Korea.

America's involvement in what was to become the Vietnam War began when President Dwight D. Eisenhower sent 500 advisors to help South Vietnam fight its communist neighbor in North Vietnam. In 1961, President John F. Kennedy sent another 14,800 advisors. In 1964, Lyndon B. Johnson received information of an attack on the U.S.S. *Maddox*, a destroyer cruising in the Gulf of Tonkin. President Johnson requested that Congress pass the Tonkin Gulf resolution, which permitted him to send troops to Vietnam and double the monthly quota of the draft. The United States government had begun to register all 18-year-old males for the draft in 1948.

In 1974, Mayor John Gregorio presented a key to the city to Linden war veteran George T. Coker, who was shot down over North Vietnam on August 27, 1966, and was a prisoner of war for eight years. Coker, who was promoted to full lieutenant during his captivity, was presented with six awards in a ceremony held at North Island Naval Station in San Diego, California: the Navy Cross, a Silver Star, two Bronze Stars, the Legion of Merit, and a Navy Commendation. Another

Vietnam prisoner of war was Alan Kroboth, a navigator in the U.S. Marines and a graduate of Linden High School's Class of 1965.

Charles Hemenway Jr., also a member of the Class of 1965, spent four tours in Vietnam as an Airborne Ranger. He was awarded a Bronze Star with "V" device for valor, as well as a Purple Heart. Charles was the son of Charles Hemenway Sr., Linden's celebrated veteran grand marshal of the World War II parade. Both father and son now reside in Florida.

The Linden men who died in the service of their country during the Vietnam War include William J. Beksi, Thomas G. Danowski, George T. Farawell, Jeffrey C. Hahn, Ronald W. Knosky, Eugene Law, Mikolaw Melnyk, Otto J. Ostenfeld, Peter W. Scott, Franklin M. Tunick, Ronald L. Warnett, Edward T. West, David R. Wienckoski, Maurice O'Calahan, Walter T. Krizanowski, and Jeffrey L. Scheller.

April and May of 1973 was an exciting time in Linden, welcoming home three POWs of the Vietnam War with three separate receptions as they were released from captivity and returned to Linden. George T. Coker arrived back in Linden first on April 21, 1973. Highly decorated, he was a prisoner of war for seven years. Marine First Lieutenant Alan Kroboth returned on April 26, 1973. Army Staff Sergeant Robert A. Tabb returned in May 1973. The ceremonies included Carol Williams singing the National Anthem, prayers by Reverend Robert Bryant and Father Kenneth Mayer, the presentation of the key to the city by Mayor Gregorio, and a resolution from the Union County Freeholders.

Lieutenant Kroboth, son of Mr. and Mrs. Joseph F. Kroboth, resided on E. Edgar Road and attended School No. 2, Soehl Junior High School, and Linden High school, where he was an avid basketball player and was named Athlete of the Year in 1965. He also graduated from the Citadel in Charleston, South Carolina. Kroboth was a navigator shot down just below the demilitarized zone in July 1972; he stayed at "Plantation Gardens" before moving into the now infamous "Hanoi Hilton."

Tabb attended Linden schools and graduated from Soehl Junior High School before moving to Georgia. Sergeant Tabb enlisted in the Army in 1965 and returned to Linden just before leaving for active duty. He had been a prisoner of the Viet Cong since April 1970. Tabb, son of Mrs. Lucille McAlpin, resided on Union Street.

In a special award ceremony held on May 10, 2000, at the Lawrenceville Armory, Major General Paul J. Glazar, the adjutant general for the State of New Jersey, presented the New Jersey Distinguished Service Medal, the state's top military award, to 135 state residents who were combat veterans of World War II, Korea, Vietnam, or the Persian Gulf War. The following Linden men were so honored that day:

> Petty Officer Second Class John J. Hansen, United States Navy
> Seaman First Class Leo Paserba, United States Navy
> Technician Fifth Grade John Prechodzen, United States Army
> Private First Class Daniel J. Rotunno, United States Army (posthumous)

On September 11, 2001, terrorists bent on suicide and mass murder struck at the heart of the nation's military and financial centers as part of a closely timed series of attacks. At 8:45 a.m., American Airlines Flight 11 out of Boston, Massachusetts, crashed into the north tower of the World Trade Center in New York City. At 9:03 a.m., United Airlines Flight 175 from Boston crashed into the south tower. By 10:30 a.m., the twin 110-story towers had fallen, darkening the sky with ash and smoke. In New York City alone, more than 2,000 had died. Then, at 10:05 a.m., American Airlines Flight 77 crashed into the Pentagon, destroying an entire wing of the United States government's military command center and killing both military and civilian personnel.

Finally, United Airlines Flight 93 crashed in a field in Shanksville, Somerset County, Pennsylvania, after setting out from Newark, New Jersey, for San Francisco. The plane had turned mid-flight and was headed toward Washington, D.C. when it went down with 4 hijackers aboard, as well as 37 passengers, 2 pilots, and 5 flight attendants. Linden resident Wanda A. Green was one of the flight attendants.

Wanda had been a flight attendant for 29 years and had also worked at the Northstar Realty in South Orange. An elder of Linden Presbyterian Church, she had planned to visit her mother and twin sister, living outside San Fransisco, during this trip. Her former husband is a retired detective living in Connecticut. Her daughter Jennifer, a genetics student at Rutgers University, said that she and

GEORGE DORIN. Dorin was a rifleman, private first class in the 35th Infantry Division. He was also a Prisoner of War from the Battle of the Bulge. (Courtesy MaryAnn Dorin.)

her 18-year-old brother Joseph, a criminal justice student at Fairleigh Dickinson University, were concerned about their mother's flights when they were younger but had developed a false sense of security as they got older—"We didn't think anything like this would happen."

Days after September 11, rising smoke where the World Trade Center towers had once stood was still visible from the Tremley section of Linden. The events of that day affected not only the United States, but the entire world. In the four hijacked jetliners, 266 passengers and crewmembers lost their lives. Thousands more on the ground are dead, and many are still missing.

FAMOUS WAR-TIME PICTURE. This image was widely circulated by the press and is entitled "Linden," depicting a loyal canine looking wistfully after his master, a soldier who had just left on a troop train after a furlough at the home of Charles Buchar on West Linden Avenue. After that day, canine instinct impelled "Linden" to give a farewell visit and longing look to all men in khaki who left from Linden. A freelance New York photographer took the picture and Irene LaFortun, a journalism major at the New Jersey College for Women at the time, supplied the story. (Courtesy Linden VFW.)

12. EARLY INDUSTRY

Local industries in Linden were first developed on the farm. The soil was intensely cultivated though farms were smaller here than they were in the western portion of the state. Wheat was the main cash crop, and vegetables were raised for home consumption. Corn was not raised extensively, but other grains were fairly abundant, and potatoes were not planted extensively until after 1750. The fruits of this vicinity, noted for their variety and excellence, included apples and peaches, which could be dried for winter use. Apples were also used to make cider and brandy.

In order to farm, land first had to be cleared, and in some cases, trees and brush were burned down as the easiest method of removal. Sometimes this wood, however, was taken to sawmills in the vicinity to be turned into lumber for building purposes.

As seen from early wills in New Jersey Archives, some of the early settlers were tradesmen as well as farmers. Thomas Cramer, John Shotwell, Peter and Thomas Morss, and John and William Thompson were all carpenters. Joseph Halsey and John Winans were weavers. John Wood was a clothier. Robert Morss, William Johnson, and John Thomas were tailors. John Wilson was a blacksmith. Thomas Clarke was both a carpenter and haberdasher. John Clarke was a merchant mason. James Wood was a shipwright. Cattle raising was another task taken on by some settlers.

Even back then, roads were needed to motivate commerce. The Middlesex and Essex Turnpike, a toll road in the middle of Linden, was built in 1806 to a Judge Lawrence's house in Newark from the New Brunswick Bridge. It would later become part of the Pennsylvania Railroad. The road now known as Edgar Road credits its own existence to this toll road. Because of their adversity to paying the toll demanded on the turnpike, the farmers of Linden began using a short road that ran from Elizabeth into Morse Mill Road (and gradually formed into a highway) parallel to the turnpike.

This road was called the Edgar Shunpike. "Shunpike" was an apt description of the situation of the time. In later years, Edgar Road became part of what was known as Route 25 and now as Route 1. This superhighway extends from Maine to the Florida Keys.

Another short stretch of road running parallel to the railroad tracks is today known as Linden Avenue, a very old road that connected Elizabeth and Woodbridge. It is quite likely that when the Middlesex and Essex Turnpike was built, it utilized part of the road that is now Linden Avenue. Although there is no record of the construction of Linden Avenue, research indicates that it was built in the seventeenth century.

Today, Linden benefits by its accessibility from both the New Jersey Turnpike at Exit 13 and the Garden State Parkway at Exit 135. Crews broke ground for the construction of the New Jersey Turnpike in January 1950, and an industrial access to the Tremley Point area of Linden is being considered currently. The Garden State Parkway is operated by the New Jersey Highway Authority, which was established by the New Jersey State Legislature in 1952. Both roadways are imperative to Linden's commerce.

In the years following the Civil War, many suburban communities were being developed in New Jersey. Land and improvement companies were incorporated, and Linden was heavily advertised to the commuter population. The city was described in one advertisement as a "pretty little village" in New Jersey with "about 100 houses and a population of nearly 500 people. No more finely shaded street can be found in this section of the country than Wood Avenue in the summer."

An 1895 brochure entitled "Property for Sale at the Real Estate Agency of H.W. Gesner, Linden, New Jersey" was written to lure New York and Newark businessmen and their families, who wished to get away from the hustle and bustle of city life. Stressing the ease of commuting to New York City, the brochure explained, "There are trains to and from to accommodate all classes of people." There were no businesses or factory sections mentioned in the brochure on Linden; in fact, commercial establishments were virtually nonexistent.

The South Wood Avenue area, near the Pennsylvania Railroad station of Linden Township, boasted a business section of just three or four stores, carrying only grocery staples and notions, on the main thoroughfare. There were only two stores on North Wood Avenue in the borough section: Hilliard's Drug Store, which stood near the corner of Elizabeth Avenue, and Gesner's General Store, which was located on the corner of Blancke Street on the front property of the present-day city hall. Furniture, clothing, and specialty items had to be purchased in Elizabeth, Newark, or New York.

There were certainly no parking problems for these earlier shoppers; all that was necessary was a hitching post for horses and a rack for bicycles. During the early 1900s, other small stores opened in the train station area on South Wood Avenue. Bartlemus Valvano, an Italian immigrant, established Linden's first Italian-American store, located at 110 South Wood Avenue. These owner-operated establishments typically had living quarters behind or above the store. H.W. Gesner realized some extra revenue by renting his third floor to the Knights of Pythias and later to the first volunteer fire department. Gesner described Linden in a brochure as follows:

INTERSECTION OF ELIZABETH AND WOOD AVENUES, 1920. This image was taken from the train platform. (Courtesy Shirley Stuewe.)

We offer for sale at Linden more than one hundred plots of land. . . . Some of them are on Wood Avenue, an avenue 80 feet wide, running the length of the town and paved macadamized from the depot to the county road or St. George's Avenue. Some of these plots are on Elizabeth Avenue within three minutes walk of the railroad station. Others are on Linden Avenue, and many others are on the property of Reverend Oscar Gesner. . . . These plots are all located in the most desirable parts of the village, and are well drained, high land, and range in price from $150 to $750 per lot. Title Perfect and guaranteed.

The Gesner brochure offered a plot on Price Street containing a "huge and comfortable house, with a bathroom and furnace, lot 100 feet by 200 feet deep small barn, etc.; well stocked with fruit. Price $5,500." The brochure also mentioned a "comfortable cottage" with stable and outbuildings, at $4,000, that was "in every respect desirable for a small family." There was also an $18,000 "three-story and French Roof House with twelve rooms besides bath room, store room, butler's pantry."

After the division of Linden into the borough and township, the development of the community continued. Soon, the same real estate companies that were selling plots in the residential areas also became interested in locating new industries in Linden.

MERCHANTS INDUSTRIES. Located at 104 East Elizabeth Avenue, the building was later the home of Park Plastics, which manufactures tons of plastic collectible toys. (Courtesy UCHS.)

Tremley was home to Cities Service Oil Company. Crude oil arrived in ships to be converted into more than 50 products, ranging from road oils to very firm industrial asphalts used for roofing and siding. The capacity of asphalt production in this ultra-modern refinery amounts to 400,000 tons a year. Gasoline and fuel oils are byproducts at the asphalt refinery. In addition to asphalt refining, this location was the Cities Service terminal. H. Roy Wheeler and Myles McManus, both Linden mayors, were employed here. After serving as mayor, Wheeler returned to Cities Service and resumed his duties in the sales department.

Another industrial beginning came in 1907, when the American Cyanamid Company bought Warners Works on Tremley Point Road. The company started with only a single product of nitrogen for fertilizing but soon became one of the largest chemical producers and researchers in the world. Cyanamid's large plant in Linden was built in 1916, and through the years, its buildings were spread over nearly 30 acres of waterfront property. The plant began making oil additives to prolong the life of motor oils, fumigants and insecticides, aluminum sulfate to safeguard drinking water, rubber accelerators to make automobile tires last longer, and sulfuric acid for use in the manufacturing of an unlimited number of products.

Weldon Materials, located at 2000 Marshes Dock Road, is a family business that was established in the 1890s. Weldon Materials and its subsidiaries have continually been leaders in the construction industry.

Thorn-Wilmerding Corporation, a division of Weldon Materials, operated a ready-mixed concrete and mason materials business on the Rahway River at the foot of Marshes Dock Road. This plant is situated on land that was once part of the farm owned by Stuart C. Marsh. In those days, the land held various farm buildings, a tree-lined lane, and a dock from which boating, fishing, and bathing were enjoyed. Much of the Marsh farm produce was shipped by boat to New York City. In 1919, P.W. Lambert, with assistance of John Fedor, leased this property from the Marsh estate. The dock facilities were improved so that cinders, sand, gravel, and crushed stone could be transported on barges. Lambert took title to the property in 1931 and started the ready-mixed concrete phase of the business. However, the Depression took its toll and the business was dormant for several years. In 1936, the facility was acquired by D.A. Thorn and H.B. Wilmerding, and operations were resumed. Then, Weldon Materials, which operated two other ready-mixed concrete plants, two blacktop plants, and a stone quarry, purchased the business in 1950. Weldon currently operates ten hot-mixed plants, five ready-mixed plants, and three contractor supply yards; they also own a trap rock quarry in Watchung and a granite quarry in Lake Hopatcong.

MELLOR'S SERVICE STATION, MARCH 21, 1931. Located at 221 North Wood Avenue, they sold Esso gas for 18¢ a gallon while the other fuel was only 15¢. (Courtesy Doris Henel.)

Since 1946, Weldon Asphalt Corporation has been another division of Weldon Materials. Also located on Marshes Dock Road, the business has engaged in the manufacture of blacktop for roads and driveways.

Adam Cook's Sons, Inc. was founded in 1868 in Albany, New York, and the company came to Linden in 1926, occupying the old Transatlantic Chemical plant at North Stiles Street. The original structure had been rebuilt and enlarged. The company's product line was extended to include a full line of metalworking lubricants and specialties for industry.

Rheem Manufacturing Company was located at 1701 West Edgar Road where K-Mart now stands. A galvanizing operation in Emeryville, California, in the 1930s marked the beginning of the business, which supplied American homes and industry with a variety of products from 17 plants across the country. In addition, 32 plants in 16 other countries supply the people of the free world with a variety of home conveniences and industrial supplies. The plant in Linden produced steel containers (in 1-gallon to 60-gallon sizes) used by food, chemical, paint, and petroleum companies from upstate New York to North Carolina.

Gordon's Dry Gin was established in 1769 by Alexander Gordon, and today, the juniper-based beverage is still made to the same original and highly secret recipe. It was once said, "London came to Linden in 1934." Every drop produced by the company was once distilled, bottled, and shipped by the 300 employees at the Gordons' home in Linden, New Jersey, although Gordon's Dry Gin Co. Ltd. has since moved from the city. The company is currently owned by United Distillers.

GIRLS JUST WANT TO HAVE FUN. These ladies posed outside Gordon's Gin during a break in 1938. (Courtesy Banasiak family.)

BACK, BOOST, AND BUY IN LINDEN. *This chamber of commerce decal urged citizens to support their local industries. (Courtesy Richard Koziol.)*

A division of the Coca-Cola Company, Tenco, located at 720 West Edgar Road, came into being because ten coffee roasting firms realized that research was the key to the future of the coffee business. Tenco was organized and performed coffee bean analysis, doing research to learn the secrets of coffee aroma and flavor. Green coffee beans, received from all over the world, were carefully roasted and checked every few minutes, day and night, to ensure proper development. The roasted beans were then ground for the coffee brewers. The substance that came out of the coffee brewer was a rather thick liquid, which underwent a number of further quality checks. It was then conveyed to the giant dryers contained within seven-story-high cylinders. The liquid entered the top of the dryer under pressure and, on its trip to the bottom, had the water removed. The powder that emerged was instant coffee.

KASTNER BREAD WAGON. The store was located on the 100 block of North Wood Avenue and was followed in that location by Daily Photo. (Courtesy Robert Kastner.)

Morey LaRue Top Laundry and Dry Cleaning, located at 2400 East Linden Avenue, was founded as a partnership in 1890 in Easton, Pennsylvania, by Mahlon Morey and William LaRue. The firm expanded to the Linden-Elizabeth area three years later. Directing Morey LaRue's operations were Frank Scott Jr., who became president in 1942, and Mahlon M. Scott, vice president and secretary, who was named general manager in December 1960. The firm's other officers included Louis W. Haviland and Lester H. Wright, vice presidents; Albert L. Ward, treasurer; and Agnes M. Lauer, assistant treasurer. Mahlon Scott is the president of the company today.

The company has also received worldwide recognition for its laundry and dry cleaning leadership, and many important improvements in machinery and methods have been tested and perfected at Morey LaRue's main Linden plant on Lidgerwood Avenue. Laundrymen and dry cleaners from all over the world frequently visit Morey LaRue to study its equipment and procedures. In addition to its Linden plant, Morey LaRue also operates large laundry and cleaning plants in Morristown and Easton, Pennsylvania.

Farber Brothers' Lumber Co. Inc., located at 1025 West St. Georges Avenue, was established by Theodore Farber after his discharge from the Navy in World War I. Farber began with a sand and mason yard next to the Pennsylvania Railroad tracks. From there, he expanded into the lumber business in Roselle. His sons, Leonard and William, carried on the family tradition of service.

The insurance business of William G. Palmero, Inc. at 441 North Wood Avenue, was established by Bill Sr. in 1922. Bill Jr., a graduate of Drake University, joined his father in 1949, specializing in insurance underwriting. Alfred Palmero, a graduate of Rutgers University, joined the firm in 1955 and specializes in real estate brokerage. The company provides complete services in the fields of insurance and real estate.

142

Daily Photo Service, with two locations at 117 North Wood Avenue and West Price Street, was founded in 1950 and offered complete photographic services to Linden. Daily's specialty was fast service on developing and printing and the processing of all color movie, 35 millimeter, and roll film. They also carried a huge inventory of photographic equipment and supplies. Unfortunately, the owners retired in 1996 and the business closed, but in its existence, Daily Photo was responsible for many of the invaluable photographs held today in the city's archives.

John Stephenson began building carriages in New York City in 1831 and produced the world's first street car a year later. It was the famous John Mason built for the pioneer New York & Harlem Railroad. Still, Stephenson focused on stagecoach and omnibus production. The Stephenson plant was moved to Linden in 1898. The original buildings remain at what is currently 2515 to 2541 Brunswick Avenue, in the Bayway section of Linden. In 1904, Stephenson was acquired by the J.G. Brill Company of Philadelphia, although production continued under the Stephenson name. However, the plant was never equipped with machinery for the manufacture of steel cars and Brill discontinued car building at Elizabeth in 1917. At that time, it was the oldest car builder in the world. These buildings were occupied for many years by the Simmons Bedding Company, which is currently a warehouse, but some rail remains in the floor.

Elizabeth-Town Stage Wagon.

THE subscribers take this method to inform the public that they have erected a S T A G E W A G O N, with four horses, suitable for carrying passengers and their baggage from Elizabeth Town to Princeton, there to meet Mr. Gershom Johnson's Flying Stage.—This Stage will set out every Monday and Thursday mornings, at eight o'clock, from Doctor Winans's tavern in Elizabeth Town, dine at Drake's in Brunswick, lodge at Mr. Bergen's in Princeton, exchange passengers, return in the morning, and complete the journey in two days from Elizabeth Town to Philadelphia.

The Price for each passenger, from Elizabeth-Town, to Philadelphia to be Four Hard Dollars, or the value thereof in other money; and the like sum for 150 weight of baggage. ——No run goods to be admitted in this Stage on any account.
ICHABOD GRUMMAN, Junr.
JAMES DRAKE.

ADVERTISEMENT IN NEW JERSEY JOURNAL OF OCTOBER 30, 1781. This stagecoach, leaving from Doc Winans Tavern of Elizabethtown, was a common sight before the days of the Pennsylvania Railroad and Central Railroad. (Courtesy UCHS.)

143

13. A GLIMPSE AT COMMUNITY ORGANIZATIONS

Across the country, countless organizations and societies have been formed to provide assistance, education, companionship, and enjoyment to residents in every community. In Linden, many local clubs and fraternal organizations, some known specifically as "service" clubs, have contributed and continue to contribute an enormous amount to the general welfare of the city. Political groups have been organized to support the causes and platforms of the Independent, Democratic, and Republican parties, and many cultural groups have found a home in Linden as well. Though space precludes listing all these fine organizations and their worthwhile projects, what follows is a taste of the public spirit that is found throughout Linden.

The Linden Country Club had its headquarters in what was first the Linden Casino, built by Walther Luttgens in 1870. It served as the community center, a place for recreation and social activities, for both the township and borough of Linden in the early days, before the club was disbanded in 1937. Life revolved around the country club; it was the place for dances and card parties, tennis matches, and billiard games. In the early days, too, the club sponsored a baseball team. At one time, the Rotary Club met at the country club building at 312 Luttgen Place, as did the Junior Order of United American Mechanics. Two generations enjoyed the facilities of the country club, and members included former mayor H.B. Hardenburg, William Joseph, Leo McDonagh, Joseph Neubauer, Henry and Fred Blancke, Clarence H. Smith, William Hill, Ralph S. Swinton, Receiver of Taxes Herbert D. Banta, Frank R. Anderson, D.A. Howell, Henry Dabb, John P. Mahar, Tom Sullivan, A.C. Baldwin, Garrett Maye, Halle Hardenburg, and C. Dudley Blancke. The building still stands today as the home of the Moose Lodge.

The Loyal Order of Moose, Linden Lodge, No. 913 was organized in Linden in 1926, and the group held its meetings on Mitchell Avenue before purchasing the Linden Country Club on Luttgen Place in 1937. The lodge sponsored a scout troop and a baseball team in the City League, gives an award to outstanding youth of Linden in leadership, and consistently supports the Halloween Parade Committee. The Women of the Moose, a ladies auxiliary organized in 1929, provides a $150 scholarship for education and a Sea Scout's Mothers Club.

LINDEN COUNTRY CLUB.
From left to right are Edna
Mellor, Gladys Archer,
Margaret Swinton, Gladys
Croucher, Jennie Mason, and
Gladys Gaub, who showed up
for this costumed Halloween
party on October 30, 1921.
(Courtesy Doris Henel.)

The Linden Chamber of Commerce evolved from a small but extremely active organization known as the Wood Avenue Improvement Association and played an important role in the development of the city. In fact, the movement for the consolidation of the township and the borough into the city of Linden was spearheaded by the Wood Avenue group, and the organization of the chamber soon followed. Jules Verner was elected its first president, succeeding Coloman Danninger, whose spirit provided much of the energy behind the Wood Avenue Improvement Association. Other members of the board were John Sweet (secretary), John J. Molson (vice president), John Fedor (treasurer), N.M. Palermo, Albert Cooley, H.D. Banta, Leon Watson, George Bauer, Forrest Farmer, and Fred McGillvray. These men were the driving force behind the efforts to improve Linden's commerce. The chamber supported projects such as the construction of a community building, a community hospital, a public swimming pool, a city incinerator, a municipal dock, and a city-owned water plant. It also pushed to improve the Rahway River.

In the early 1920s, a group of public-spirited Americans of Italian descent began to meet for social gatherings, and soon, several of the men decided to form an organization that would benefit their community. On December 11, 1922, they incorporated as the American-Italian Mutual Association. The association sponsored activities that contributed to the cultural education of and interaction between its members and the community at large. The American-Italian Association rented meeting facilities until September 1955, when the group purchased property at 101 East Blancke Street. The limited space and the growing need for repairs at this first location spurred the members to look for better facilities. The club was relocated to 800 Roselle Street in 1963. The Women's Auxiliary was organized in 1960.

In addition to the American-Italian Mutual Association, Linden residents have formed a number of clubs dedicated to the cultural diversity of their community. They have included the following organizations: Ancient Order of Hibernians and Auxiliary, Daughters of Scotia, German American Citizens Club, Hungarian Round Table Charitable Association, Lithuanian Liberty Park, American Lithuanian Citizens Club, Federation of Polish Societies, Linden Falcon Nest, Mme. Pilsudski Social Group, Pulaski Parade Committee, Polish Benefit Society, Polish Women's Alliance Group, "Sztandag-Wolnosci" Group, Slovak American Citizens Association, and Slovak National Benefit Society.

In the fall of 1920, several Masonic brethren formed the Craftsmen's Club of Linden, which was officially established in January 1921. After many meetings, a committee was appointed to procure the necessary information relative to the formation of a Masonic lodge, and in December 1921, the Grand Lodge of New

CRAFTSMEN'S CLUB. The club was originally built as the Peoples Lyceum, a social hall for the Jewish Community. It was also used for services of Saint Paul's Lutheran Church and the Baptist Church. (Courtesy L. Yeats.)

Jersey was petitioned for a warrant to do Masonic work. On Wednesday, January 25, 1922, the grand master of the Masons for the state of New Jersey met with the brethren in the old borough hall at Wood Avenue and Blancke Street and presented a dispensation empowering the group to engage in Masonic work.

The first regular meeting of the Cornerstone Lodge took place on January 27, 1922, at the borough hall. William M. Watson was the first acting master. The first conferring of degrees was held on February 24, 1922, and on May 8, 1922, the lodge was duly constituted as Cornerstone Lodge No. 229, Free and Accepted Masons, in the old Kean Building on Broad Street in Elizabeth (the later site of the Woolworth Building). On May 12, 1922, the third degree was conferred on Henry B. Hardenburg, who had served as borough mayor for 21 consecutive years. The Craftsmen's Club was purchased on Elizabeth Avenue in 1923. Through the years, the group has provided its facilities to the members of St. Paul's Lutheran Church and to the Baptist Church for worship, and the first meeting for the organization of the B'nai B'rith Lodge was held in the Craftsmen's Club.

The Recreation Commission, established by Mayor Myles J. McManus during the Depression years of the 1930s, has provided a well-rounded recreational program for both young and old alike. Frank Krysiak was the commission's superintendent from 1936 to 1976. Under his guidance and that of the five-member Recreation Commission, a varied program was offered year-round; the commission operated playgrounds and day camps in the summer and community centers in the winter. It also sponsored many leagues and special units, including hobby clubs and other groups, as well as Milk Bar dances during the 1950s and 1960s. Through the years, adult education classes and special courses of instruction for children in art, dancing, sports, computers, and other fields have taken place. Thousands of people annually still take advantage of the facilities provided by the commission, which is one of the most active of the city departments. Alfred A. Volpe became the department's superintendent in 1976 and holds the position to the present day.

In 1950, the Linden Halloween Committee was formed and began to sponsor a variety of festivities around that holiday. Individuals, organizations, and schools created lavish floats for annual parades in which many local and professional marching bands also participated. Youngsters were given awards for creativity in costuming and artwork. Storefronts on Wood Avenue were painted for the season, and dances were held as part of the annual event. The group, sponsored by the recreation department, is still active today.

Recreation is a necessity in every community. The Linden Children's Camp Fund was founded in 1939 to provide wholesome summer vacations for deserving children who could not otherwise afford them. Doctors and nurses volunteered and the VFW provided lunches.

The Knights of Columbus was founded in 1882 by a 29-year-old parish priest, Father Michael J. McGivney, in the basement of St. Mary's Church in New

MR. ALFRED E. NOGI AND THE HIGHLAND AVENUE SCHOOL NO. 10 PTA. They are planting one of 17 trees donated to the school grounds in 1960. For the very first Halloween Parade, the school was represented with a Highland Scottish Dancer theme with Shirley Stires as chairperson.

Haven, Connecticut. Today, more than a century later, the Knights of Columbus has become the largest lay organization in the Catholic Church. The order has been called "the strong right arm of the Church" and has been praised by popes, presidents, and other world leaders for its support of the church, programs of evangelization and Catholic education, civic involvement, and aid to those in need. As recently as 1992, Mother Teresa of Calcutta praised the Knights in a speech on the occasion of her reception of the first Knights of Columbus Gaudium et Spes Award.

Linden Council No. 2859 of the Knights of Columbus received its charter in 1942 and met at St. Elizabeth's Church and the Lithuanian Hall on Mitchell Avenue. The first Grand Knight was Patrick Hennessy. In 1948, the Ladies Auxiliary was formed with Evelyn Roden Beck as president.

One of the landmarks of Linden is the Knights of Columbus shrine, dubbed "Our Lady of the Highway" by Reverend Kozlowski of St. Theresa's Church and located at the tip of the Columbian property at the corner of Elizabeth Avenue and Park Avenue. The shrine, designed by Al Novi, was originally built in 1960, and Joseph La Placa and William Flynn laid the brick, cemented, and completed the tile work. George Sweet needed a crane to set the statue, which had been imported from Italy, in place. Father Miller and Father Mulvany blessed the shrine upon its completion. In early 1988, vandals broke the statue, but the shrine was repaired and a new statue ordered. On September 19, 1988, Father Miller and Bishop McCarrick rededicated and blessed the shrine.

The Lions Club met at the Lynwood tavern on West St. Georges Avenue. To this day, the organization continues to raise money for the blind and for sight conservation efforts, supplying glasses and medical attention in cases of need. Their work benefits many programs, including the Lions eye bank, Union County Blind Association, St. Joseph's School for the Blind, and Camp Marcella.

Thousands of Linden's children have been active in the Girl Scouts and Boy Scouts since the first troops were established throughout the city. Scout work is also an interest close to the hearts of many Linden adults, who spend many hours guiding this activity. In 1955, Doris J. Henel, a past president of Washington Rock Girl Scout Council (WRGSC) and a present troop organizer at the United Methodist Church, wrote the following about the history of scouting in Linden:

LINDEN LIONS. *The Linden Lions was chartered in 1945. From left to right are Anthony Manuzza, Stephen Orlando, Charles Valvano Jr., Chris Homswold, Francis De Stephan, Ralph Black, Al Kalla, Edward Cooper, Ed McCarthy, Everett Copeland, Charles Valvano Sr., William Dorozin, Helmuth Breisser, Dr. Samuel Trask, Reverend Kenneth Watles, Edward Rapp, Joseph Add, Matthew Malinoski, Wilbur Pipper, Reverend Robert Cunningham, Stanley Bojak, Warren Malpas, Dominick Harold Roberts, Stanley Bojak, William La Monte, John Fitspatrick, Colonel Howell Hodgkins, Martin Wojak, John Kling, Nick Palermo, and George Sweet. (Courtesy Mrs. Dominick Caruso.)*

Girl Scouting became official in this country when Juliette Low signed a charter on March 12, 1912. Before that date, in Linden, the Campfire Girls, and Boy Scout Troop met in the Methodist Church between 1910 and 1912. In the early 1920s the first Girl Pansy Troop #1 was established by Mrs. J. Frank Miska, and they met in the Reformed Church. Mrs. Henry G. Nulton was also one of the first leaders and spent many, many years very involved in Girl Scouting in Linden.

Girl Scout and Boy Scout troops were sponsored by churches, synagogues, and schools east of St. Georges Avenue. The first memorial troop was Troop #30, sponsored by the Blancke Street Synagogue and later by the new synagogue at the corner of Orchard Terrace and St. Georges Avenue. The first leader was Mrs. Mona Glasston Kriv, the daughter of Dr. Glasston.

The first established summer camping began for the Girl Scout Council when Camp Lou Henry Hoover was opened at Liddell's Pond in Mendham on land donated by N. Brady, the son of Diamond Jim Brady, who originally owned the land. The camp included 16 sleeping tents and one cook tent loaned by the Elizabeth National Guard, and water supplies came from a natural spring. Camp Lou Henry Hoover is now located on Swartswood Lake and is rated by the state as one of the best camps in New Jersey.

Doris Henel also quoted a letter written by Mrs. J. Frank Miska, the founder of Girl Scouting in Linden, on the 50th anniversary of Scouting in Linden. Henel's letter reports the following:

> One Arbor Day the troop had 31 Norway maple trees planted around Linden High School on St. Georges Ave. The Union County Park Commission sent the men to plant the trees. Standard Oil sent their band to play at the ceremonies. The Forestry Department of Trenton sent a forester to speak. Through the efforts of Mrs. Miska's troop the trees were donated by merchants, factories and organizations of Linden. The troop had the opening night of the Plaza Theater for a benefit. The picture shown was "Birth of a Nation." New Jersey's Governor Moore attended the benefit and spoke. Tickets were sold-out and the theater was filled to capacity. Funds from this, and from cake sales and teas, bought the uniforms for the troop.

By 1961, there were 15 Boy Scout cub packs and 17 troops, totalling 1,047 members. The Explorer scouts had five units at that time as well.

The Linden Police Athletic League was organized in June 1952 by volunteers of the Linden Police Department and businessmen. In 1956, the league purchased the former Blancke Street Synagogue to serve as its headquarters and the site for many indoor activities. Since then, thousands of Linden boys and girls have taken part in PAL programs, which are funded through voluntary contributions. In addition to its police volunteers, Linden's PAL program provides qualified

BOY SCOUT TROOP #36, 1933. From left to right are (front row) leader Andrew Harvan and assistant scout leader Robert Lamont; and (back row) leader Albert Henel, Vincent Wright, and leader Vern Loveland. (Courtesy Doris Henel.)

workers and civilian volunteers to mentor and coach the children who participate. An advisory board composed of interested citizens supervises the program. Linden's PAL organization has continued to grow since its inception and will continue to do so with the help of the generous citizens, businesses, and industries of Linden.

The National Congress of Mothers was founded in 1897 to act on behalf of children in the home, at school, and in the world. The group recognized the importance of and actively promoted cooperation between parents (they strongly encouraged the participation of fathers) and teachers. The organization, today known as the Parent Teacher Association (PTA), voiced its concerns and worked tirelessly on many juvenile issues, including the need for child-labor laws. The PTA also launched a nationwide school lunch program. In 1923, School No. 1 became the first in Linden to have such an organization. Since then, every Linden public school has established a local PTA group. The important part played by these groups in the improvement of the education of Linden youths cannot be overstated.

The Rotary Club of Linden was organized on April 30, 1925, aided in part by James P. Orr, the state secretary of the Rotarians, and Adrian C. Murray, the president of the Elizabeth club. The officers elected were Harold Depew as president, Frank G. Newell as vice president, Joseph L. Newbauer as secretary, and Ralph Swinton as treasurer. In addition to these officers, the board of directors included members Henry B. Hardenburg Sr., Frank R. Anderson, and Dr. Harle P. Hough. The object of the Rotary Club, a nonpolitical and nonsectarian group, was to promote good faith among various businesses and to aid in the development of the community, state, and nation. One member, D.A. Howell, who was superintendent of the Linden schools, had a perfect attendance for 10 years, a feat for which he was presented with a Diamond Rotary Emblem. He severed his connections with the Linden Rotary Club upon his retirement from the Linden school system and subsequent move to Newton, where he soon became a member of the Newton Rotary Club.

In the past, the club has sponsored a baseball team and offered scholarships for students to attend classes during the summer sessions of the Conservatory of Music in Roselle; they have also made loans to worthy students who needed financial aid to attend college.

EARLY PAL BUILDING. *The building was at the corner of East Blancke and Maple Avenues. It was purchased from Congregation Anshe Chesed and was commonly known as the Blancke Street Synagogue. (Courtesy Edwards.)*

The League of Women Voters in Linden was organized in 1945 as part of the League of Women Voters of New Jersey and the League of Women Voters of the United States. The purpose of the league was to promote political responsibility through the informed and active participation of citizens in government, and its members worked steadily towards an understanding of the structure of government at local, state, and national levels. They urged eligible citizens to vote and provided the public with facts about the candidates.

Organized in 1946, the Linden Kiwanis Club currently meets every Thursday at the Linden United Methodist Church. Over the years, the club has granted annual college scholarships to high school seniors from Linden. Funds for this project are raised through an annual Pancake Breakfast and Spaghetti Dinner. In 1979, the first Key Club (the high school students' group of the Kiwanis Club) was organized at Linden High School, and its charter granted in 1980. In 1981, the club held its first 5-mile run and raised $3,400 through sponsorships. In 1983, Builders Clubs were started at each of the middle schools and they donated a sign to Linden High School for Edward Cooper Athletic Field. In 1993, the groups donated pediatric equipment to the Linden Volunteer Ambulance Corps and supported the pediatric trauma center at Rahway Memorial Hospital.

The Linden chapter of the Junior Chamber of Commerce was organized in 1956, but in June 1965, the national organization changed its name to the Jaycees. The organization is open to young men between the ages of 18 and 36 who want to develop themselves as leaders while contributing to the civic betterment of Linden.

From 1956 to 1961, the chapter sponsored jazz concerts for local charities, as well as youth activities, including basketball and baseball leagues. In 1957, the chapter recognized Edward Flanagan, director of the Police Athletic League, as the outstanding young man in Linden, and the New Jersey Jaycees selected him as one of the five outstanding young men in New Jersey for that same year. Due to lack of membership, the chapter became inactive in 1961.

In 1963, the Linden Jaycees was reestablished with a helping hand from the Carteret Jaycees. Members have worked at the annual Jaycee football classic, which pits the Philadelphia Eagles against the New York Giants, and have earned about $6,000 for local charities in Linden. The Jaycees also conducted a Christmas home-lighting contest, which attracted the participation of several hundred homeowners. In the summers of 1967 and 1968, the chapter sponsored weekly teenage dances at the Linden Reformed Church. From 1966 to 1968, the Linden Jaycees sponsored the Central Union County Junior Miss Pageant. The three pageants sponsored by the chapter resulted in the awarding of scholarships valued at $1,500 to the winners and runners-up.

In 1968, Linden finished 14th in the New Jersey Jaycees Parade of Chapters, and the chapter was selected by the New Jersey Jaycees for having an outstanding clean-air, clear-water project in 1967–1968. In June 1970, the Linden Jaycees sponsored its first annual Mayor's Trophy Soccer Tournament, the proceeds of which were donated to the Linden Police Athletic League and the Volunteer

LINDEN VOLUNTEER AMBULANCE CORPS. In 1979, the LVAC reached its 35th anniversary. Freeholder Thomas Long; Mayor and State Senator John T. Gregorio; and Walter Vandewater, president of LVAC, pose here. (Courtesy UCHS.)

Ambulance Corps. In April 1973, the chapter held its first Health Fair in the city, attracting some 1,500 Linden residents. The Linden Jaycees chapter is no longer a local organization.

American communities are teeming with organizations whose sole purpose is to be of civic service. The following list includes the cultural and service groups in the Linden area:

Lions Club	Kiwanis Club
League of Women Voters	League of Women Voters
Linden Bar Association	Linden Volunteer Ambulance Corps
Linden Education Foundation	Lions Club & Auxiliary
Linden Industrial Association	People for Animals
Linden Merchants Association	Rotary Club
Ministerial Association of Linden	Linden Cultural and Heritage Committee
Civic and Service	Linden Summer Playhouse
Cityline Coalition	Linden Debutante Scholarship Org.
Deborah Hilda Gould Chapter	Linden Education Association
Friends of the Linden Library	Parent Teacher Associations

American Italian Mutual Association and Ladies Auxiliary
Polish National Home
Polish Women's Alliance
General Pulaski Memorial Parade Committee
Spanish American Cultural Society
B'nai B'rith Lodges
Rotary Club
Kiwanis
BPO Elks & Auxiliary
Catholic Daughters of America
Craftsmen's Club
Exchange Club
Knights of Columbus and Auxiliary
Knights of Pythias
Masonic Temple Cornerstone Lodge
Moose Lodge & Auxiliary
Order of Eastern Star
Young Men of Zion
Homeowners Association
Linden Towers Condominium
Democratic Ward Clubs
Linden Coalition for Political Action
Linden Democratic Club and Ladies Club
Linden Republican Club
Polish American Democratic Club
Church-affiliated groups

Fifty+ Club of St. Elizabeth
Hadassah
Holy Name Societies
Intra-Faith Council of Linden
Sisterhoods
Recreation Committees & Social clubs
AARP
Senior Citizen Clubs
American Legion and Auxiliary
VFW and Auxiliary
Youth Activities
Boy Scouts of America
Catholic Youth Organization
Girl Scouts of America
Halloween Parade Committee
Mayor's Youth Commission
Police Athletic League
Ninth Ward Citizens
Summer sports and day camps

BIBLIOGRAPHY

Barber, J. and H. Howe. *Historical Collections of the State of New Jersey*. New York, NY: Tuttle, 1844.

Campbell, James W. and William S. Stryker. *Official Register of the Officers and Men of New Jersey in the Revolutionary War: With Added Digest and Revision*. Baltimore, Maryland: Clearfield Company, 1997.

Centennial Celebration Publication, "Looking Back To Look Ahead: The Story Of 100 Years Of Vigorous Growth, City Of Linden, NJ." Privately published, 1961.

Clayton, Woodford W. *History of Union and Middlesex Counties, New Jersey, with biographical sketches of many pioneers and prominent men*. Philadelphia, PA: Everts & Peck, 1882.

Cunningham, John T. *America's Main Road New Jersey*. Florham Park, NJ: Afton Publishers, 1966.

Friedlander, Paul J.C., "High Road from the Hudson to the Delaware," *New York Times,* 25 November 1951.

Gale, Joseph. *Eastern Union: The Development of a Jewish Community*. Elizabeth, NJ: The Jewish Culture Council of Eastern Union County, 1958.

Gesner, Oscar. Sermon given at the 25th anniversary of the Linden Reformed Church. Document property of Linden Reformed Church, 1898.

Gillespie, Angus Kress and Michael Aaron Rockland. *Looking for America on the New Jersey Turnpike*. New Brunswick, NJ: Rutgers University Press, 1989.

Gordon, Thomas E. *A Gazetteer of the State of New Jersey Together with a Topographical and Statistical Account of Its Counties, Towns, Villages, Canals, Rail Roads, Etc.* Trenton, NJ: Daniel Fenton, 1834.

Hatfield, Edwin F. *History of Elizabeth, New Jersey, Including the Early History of Union County*. New York: Carlton & Lanahan, 1868.

Honeyman, A. Van Doren. *History of Union County, 1664–1923*. 3 Volumes. New York, NY: New Jersey Historical Society and Lewis Historical Publishing, 1923.

Hopkins, Kathleen, "Antique Manuscript," *Home News Tribune (Central New Jersey)*, 27 February 2001.

Kull, Irving S. *New Jersey: A History*. 6 Volumes. New York, NY: American Historical Society, 1930.

Lawrence, Grace F. and Sara Light. *History of the Schools of Linden*. Linden, NJ: Linden Board of Education, 1961.

League of Women Voters. *This Is Linden*. Linden, NJ: League of Women Voters, 1961.

Lunny, Robert. *Juet's Journal: The Voyage of the Half Moon from 4 April to 7 November 1609*. Introduction by John T. Cunningham. Newark, NJ: New Jersey Historical Society, 1959.

McCormick, Richard P. *New Jersey from Colony to State, 1609–1789*. Princeton, NJ: Vanostrand Co. Inc., 1964.

McCutchen, David, trans. *The Red Record: The Wallam Olum*. Garden City Park, NY: Avery Publishing Group Inc., 1993.

Nelson, William. *Documents Relating To The Colonial History Of The State Of New Jersey, Volume XXIII. Calendar Of New Jersey Wills Vol. I. 1670–1730*. Paterson, NJ: The Press Printing & Publishing Co., 1901.

—————. *New Jersey Archives. 2nd Series, Vol. III, 1779–1780, Extracts From American Newspapers Relating To New Jersey*. Paterson, NJ: The Press Printing & Publishing Co., 1914.

Ricord, F.W. *History of Union County, New Jersey*. Newark, NJ: East Jersey History Company, 1879.

Salisbury, Rollin D. *The Glacial Geology of New Jersey, Volume V of the Final Report of the State Geologist*. Trenton, NJ: State of New Jersey, 1902.

Schwab, Armand Jr., "Built For Safety," *New York Times*, 25 November 1951.

Schenck, Herschel Lee. *Indians of New Jersey and Pennsylvania*. Self-published, 1967.

Scott, Austin, ed. *Documents Relating to the Colonial History of the State Of New Jersey. New Jersey Archives. Newspaper Extracts, Second Series. Volume V 1780–1782, By State Of New Jersey*. Paterson, NJ: State of New Jersey, 1917.

Selections from the correspondence of the Executive of New Jersey (1776–1786). Published by order of the legislature. Newark, NJ: 1848.

Shipley, Alex, et.al. *The Rediscovery of Rahway*. Rahway: Self published, 1975.

Shippey, Melda. *The Winans Family*. Bountiful, UT: Family History Publishers, 1990.

Stryker-Rodda, Kenn. *New Jersey: Digging for Ancestors in the Garden State*. Detroit, MI: Detroit Society, 1970.

—————. *New Jersey Index of Wills, Inventories, Etc. In The Office Of The Secretary Of State Prior To 1901*. Three volumes. 1912–1913, reprinted 2000.

—————. *Revolutionary Census of New Jersey*. Lambertville, NJ: Hunterdon House, 1986.

Turner, Jean-Rae. Articles appearing in *Elizabeth (New Jersey) Daily Journal* and *The Citizen* (Elizabeth, NJ), 1960–1980.

Union County Historical Society. *Proceedings of the Union County Historical Society of Union County, New Jersey, for the Years 1921, 1922, and 1923*. Elizabeth, NJ: Union County Historical Society, 1923.

Weisbrot, William and Isabelle Newmark. *The History of Linden*. Linden: WPA Project, 1938.

White, William T., ed. *The Medical Register of New York, New Jersey, and Connecticut.* New York, NY: 1883.

Yeats, Lauren Pancurak. *Images of America: Linden, New Jersey.* Charleston, SC: Arcadia Publishing, 1997.

Yesenko, Michael R. *General George Washington's Campaigns of 1775, 1776, and 1777.* Union, NJ: M.R.Y. Publishing Co. Inc., 1999.

ROSEHILL CREMATORY. Charles Lindbergh Jr., nicknamed "The Little Eagle" by the press, was cremated here. Lindbergh's baby was 20 months old when he was kidnapped on March 1, 1932 from his home in Hopewell, New Jersey. He was found 75 days later. While at the Rosehill Crematory, the press waited for the family, thinking they'd be coming from the front gates on Edgar Road. However, police officer Harry J. Weitzman escorted the Lindberghs through the side entrance located on Woodlawn Avenue at 13th Street to avoid the crowds. Bruno Richard Hauptmann was tried and convicted in 1936 for the kidnapping in Flemington, New Jersey. Refusing to confess, he went to the electric chair at Trenton State Prison on April 2, 1936. (Courtesy Yeats.)

INDEX

LINDEN CITY WOMEN'S BOWLING CHAMPIONSHIP. These "A" League Winners for Febrary and March 1941 were, from left to right, (front row) Lillian Hadley, Helen Derrig Putnam, Theo Mullmann, and Ann Healy; and (back row) Vi Mayne, Gladys Mellon, Grace Ross, and Ellen Jolly. (Courtesy Betty Lamont.)